Holt California Geometry

Homework and Practice Workbook

HOLT, RINEHART AND WINSTON
A Harcourt Education Company
Orlando • Austin • New York • San Diego • London

Printed in the United States of America

ISBN 13: 978-0-03-099022-9

10 11 12 13 1413 12 11 10
4500234790

Contents

Blackline Masters

Name ______________________________ Date ___________ Class ___________

LESSON 1-1

Practice B

Understanding Points, Lines, and Planes

Use the figure for Exercises 1–7.

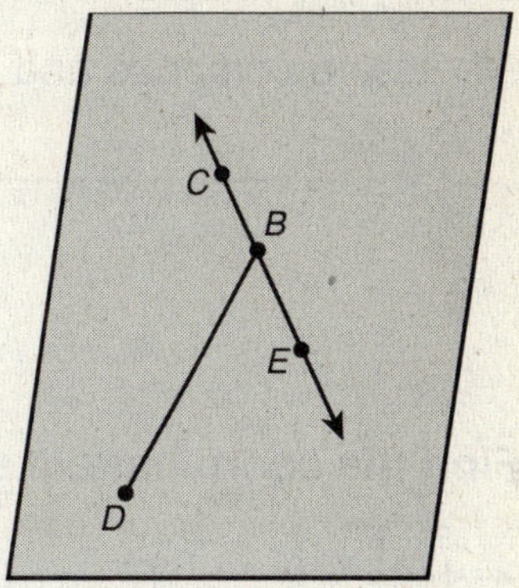

1. Name a plane. ______________________

2. Name a segment. ______________________

3. Name a line. ______________________

4. Name three collinear points.

____

5. Name three noncollinear points.

____

6. Name the intersection of a line and a segment not on the line. ______________________

7. Name a pair of opposite rays. ______________________

Use the figure for Exercises 8–11.

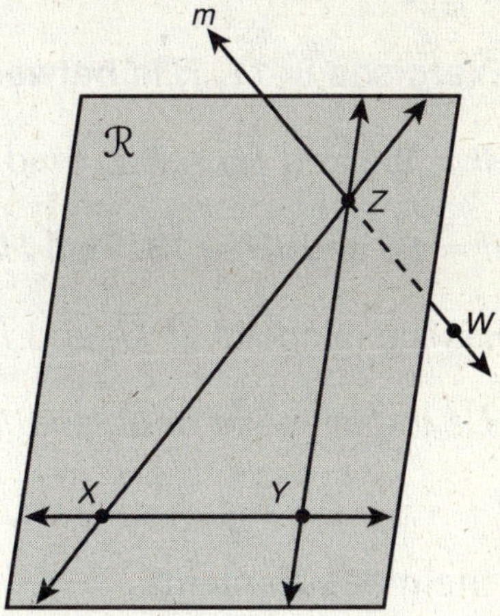

8. Name the points that determine plane ℛ.

____

9. Name the point at which line *m* intersects plane ℛ. ______________________

10. Name two lines in plane ℛ that intersect line *m*.

____

11. Name a line in plane ℛ that does not intersect line *m*. ______________________

Draw your answers in the space provided.

Michelle Kwan won a bronze medal in figure skating at the 2002 Salt Lake City Winter Olympic Games.

12. Michelle skates straight ahead from point *L* and stops at point *M*. Draw her path.

13. Michelle skates straight ahead from point *L* and continues through point *M*. Name a figure that represents her path. Draw her path.

14. Michelle and her friend Alexei start back to back at point *L* and skate in opposite directions. Michelle skates through point *M*, and Alexei skates through point *K*. Draw their paths.

Name ______________________ Date ____________ Class ____________

LESSON 1-2

Practice B

Measuring and Constructing Segments

Draw your answer in the space provided.

1. Use a compass and straightedge to construct $\overline{XY}$ congruent to $\overline{UV}$.

Find the coordinate of each point.

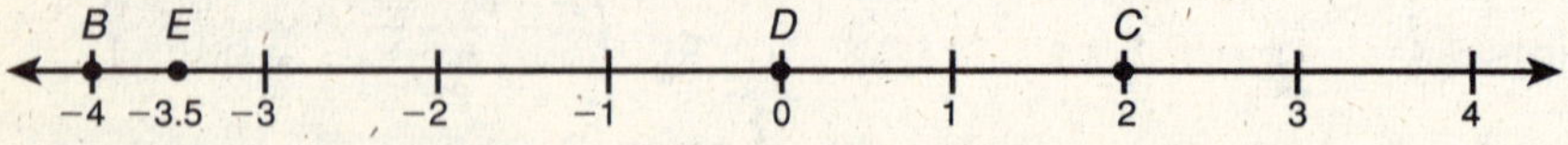

2. *D* ______ 3. *C* ______ 4. *E* ______

Find each length.

5. *BE* ______ 6. *DB* ______ 7. *EC* ______

For Exercises 8–11, *H* is between *I* and *J*.

8. $HI = 3.9$ and $HJ = 6.2$. Find *IJ*. ________

9. $JI = 25$ and $IH = 13$. Find *HJ*. ________

10. *H* is the midpoint of $\overline{IJ}$, and $IH = 0.75$. Find *HJ*. ________

11. *H* is the midpoint of $\overline{IJ}$, and $IJ = 9.4$. Find *IH*. ________

Find the measurements.

12.

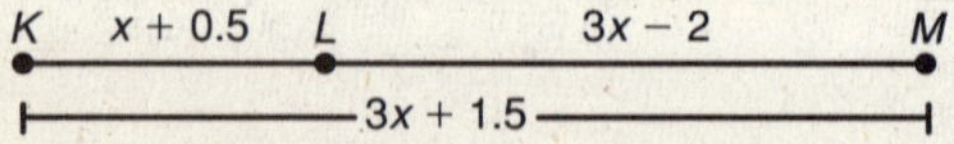

Find *LM*. ________

13. A pole-vaulter uses a 15-foot-long pole. She grips the pole so that the segment below her left hand is twice the length of the segment above her left hand. Her right hand grips the pole 1.5 feet above her left hand. How far up the pole is her right hand? ________________

Name ______________________ Date __________ Class __________

LESSON 1-3

Practice B

Measuring and Constructing Angles

Draw your answer on the figure.

1. Use a compass and straightedge to construct angle bisector $\overrightarrow{DG}$.

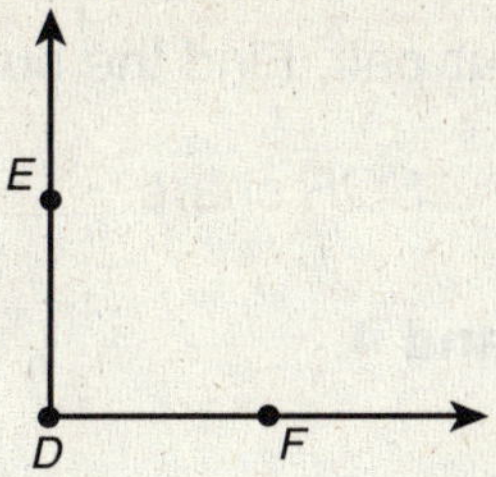

2. Name eight different angles in the figure.

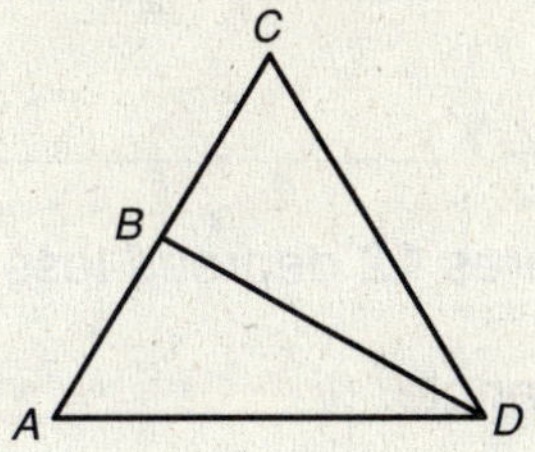

____

____

Find the measure of each angle and classify each as acute, right, obtuse, or straight.

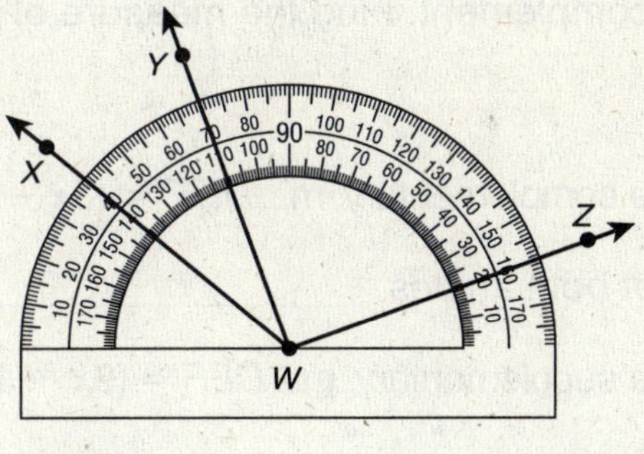

3. ∠*YWZ* ____________ 4. ∠*XWZ* ____________ 5. ∠*YWX* ____________

***T* is in the interior of ∠*PQR*. Find each of the following.**

6. m∠*PQT* if m∠*PQR* = 25° and m∠*RQT* = 11°. ________

7. m∠*PQR* if m∠*PQR* = $(10x - 7)°$, m∠*RQT* = $5x°$, and m∠*PQT* = $(4x + 6)°$. ________

8. m∠*PQR* if $\overrightarrow{QT}$ bisects ∠*PQR*, m∠*RQT* = $(10x - 13)°$, and m∠*PQT* = $(6x + 1)°$. ________

9. Longitude is a measurement of position around the equator of Earth. Longitude is measured in degrees, minutes, and seconds. Each degree contains 60 minutes, and each minute contains 60 seconds. Minutes are indicated by the symbol ′ and seconds are indicated by the symbol ″. Williamsburg, VA, is located at 76°42′25″. Roanoke, VA, is located at 79°57′30″. Find the difference of their longitudes in degrees, minutes, and seconds. ____________

10. To convert minutes and seconds into decimal parts of a degree, divide the number of minutes by 60 and the number of seconds by 3,600. Then add the numbers together. Write the location of Roanoke, VA, as a decimal to the nearest thousandths of a degree. ____________

Name ______________________ Date ___________ Class ___________

LESSON 1-4

Practice B

Pairs of Angles

1. ∠*PQR* and ∠*SQR* form a linear pair. Find the sum of their measures. ____________

2. Name the ray that ∠*PQR* and ∠*SQR* share. ____________

Use the figures for Exercises 3 and 4.

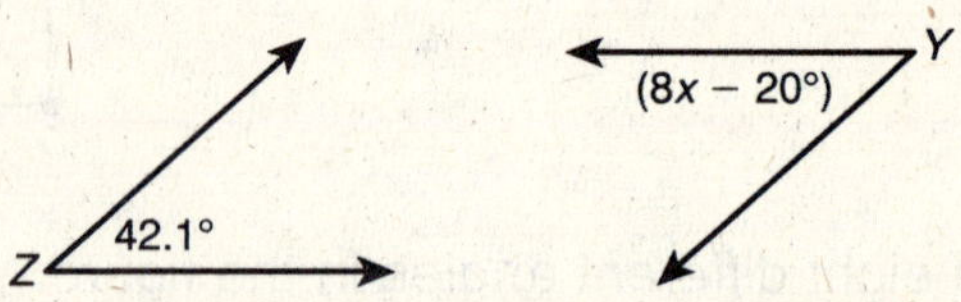

3. supplement of ∠*Z* ____________

4. complement of ∠*Y* ____________

5. An angle measures 12 degrees less than three times its supplement. Find the measure of the angle. ____________

6. An angle is its own complement. Find the measure of a supplement to this angle. ____________

7. ∠*DEF* and ∠*FEG* are complementary. m∠*DEF* = $(3x - 4)°$, and m∠*FEG* = $(5x + 6)°$. Find the measures of both angles. ____________

8. ∠*DEF* and ∠*FEG* are supplementary. m∠*DEF* = $(9x + 1)°$, and m∠*FEG* = $(8x + 9)°$. Find the measures of both angles. ____________

Use the figure for Exercises 9 and 10.

In 2004, several nickels were minted to commemorate the Louisiana Purchase and Lewis and Clark's expedition into the American West. One nickel shows a pipe and a hatchet crossed to symbolize peace between the American government and Native American tribes.

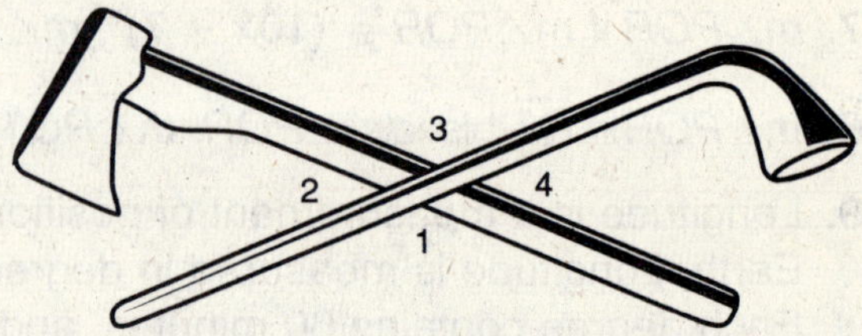

9. Name a pair of vertical angles. ____________ ____________

10. Name a linear pair of angles. ____________

11. ∠*ABC* and ∠*CBD* form a linear pair and have equal measures. Tell if ∠*ABC* is acute, right, or obtuse. ____________

12. ∠*KLM* and ∠*MLN* are complementary. $\overrightarrow{LM}$ bisects ∠*KLN*. Find the measures of ∠*KLM* and ∠*MLN*. ____________

Name ______________________ Date __________ Class __________

LESSON **1-5**

Practice B

Using Formulas in Geometry

Use the figures for Exercises 1–3.

A
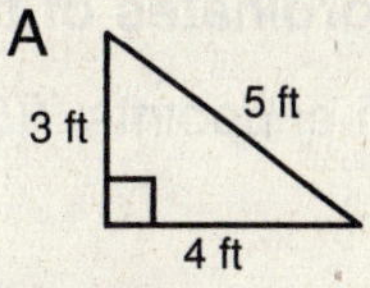

B
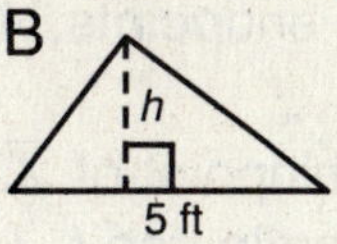

1. Find the perimeter of triangle *A*. ______________

2. Find the area of triangle *A*. ______________

3. Triangle *A* is identical to triangle *B*. Find the height *h* of triangle *B*. ______________

Find the perimeter and area of each shape.

4. square with a side 2.4 m in length

____

5. rectangle with length $(x + 3)$ and width 7

____

6. Although a circle does not have sides, it does have a perimeter. What is the term for the perimeter of a circle? ______________

Find the circumference and area of each circle.

7.
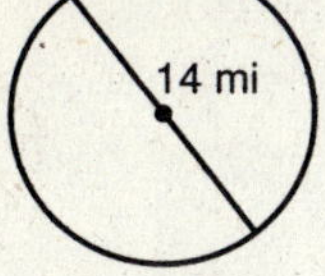

Use $\frac{22}{7}$ for π.

____

8.
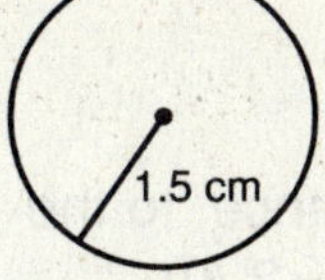

Use 3.14 for π.

____

9.
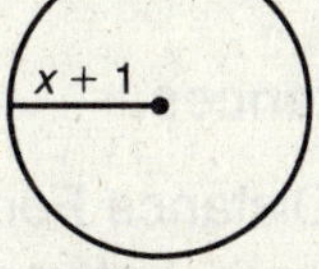

Leave π as π.

____

10. The area of a square is $\frac{1}{4}$ in^2. Find the perimeter. ______________

11. The area of a triangle is 152 m^2, and the height is 16 m. Find the base. ______________

12. The circumference of a circle is 25π mm. Find the radius. ______________

Use the figure for Exercises 13 and 14.

Lucas has a 39-foot-long rope. He uses all the rope to outline this T-shape in his backyard. All the angles in the figure are right angles.

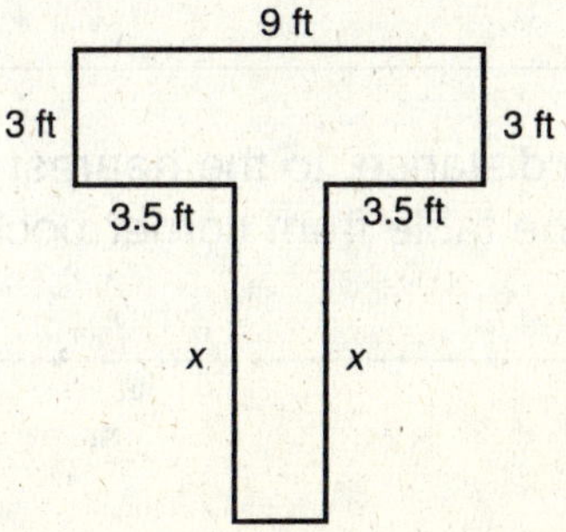

13. Find *x*. ______________

14. Find the area enclosed by the rope. ______________

Name ______________________________ Date ____________ Class ____________

LESSON 1-6

Practice B

Midpoint and Distance in the Coordinate Plane

Find the coordinates of the midpoint of each segment.

1. $\overline{TU}$ with endpoints $T(5, -1)$ and $U(1, -5)$ ____________

2. $\overline{VW}$ with endpoints $V(-2, -6)$ and $W(x + 2, y + 3)$ ____________

3. Y is the midpoint of $\overline{XZ}$. X has coordinates (2, 4), and Y has coordinates (–1, 1). Find the coordinates of Z. ____________

Use the figure for Exercises 4–7.

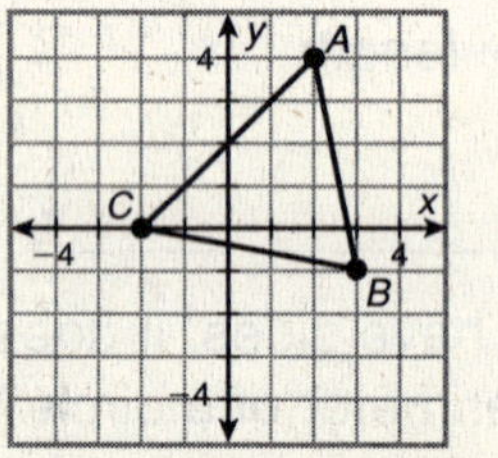

4. Find AB. ____________

5. Find BC. ____________

6. Find CA. ____________

7. Name a pair of congruent segments. ____________

Find the distances.

8. Use the Distance Formula to find the distance, to the nearest tenth, between $K(-7, -4)$ and $L(-2, 0)$. ____________

9. Use the Pythagorean Theorem to find the distance, to the nearest tenth, between $F(9, 5)$ and $G(-2, 2)$. ____________

Use the figure for Exercises 10 and 11.

Snooker is a kind of pool or billiards played on a 6-foot-by-12-foot table. The side pockets are halfway down the rails (long sides).

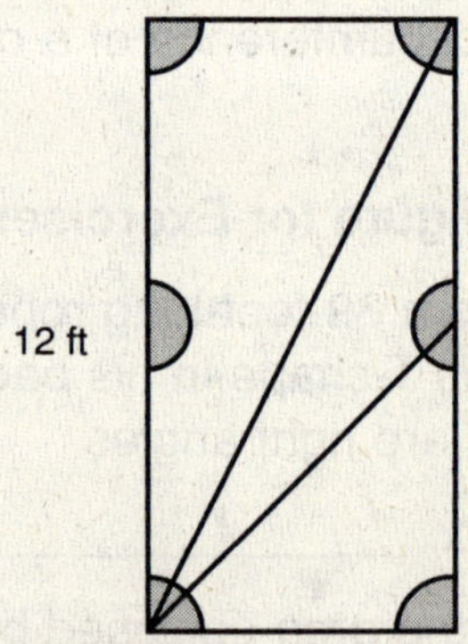

10. Find the distance, to the nearest tenth of a foot, diagonally across the table from corner pocket to corner pocket.

____

11. Find the distance, to the nearest tenth of an inch, diagonally across the table from corner pocket to side pocket.

____

Name ______________________ Date ___________ Class ___________

LESSON 1-7

Practice B

Transformations in the Coordinate Plane

Use the figure for Exercises 1–3.

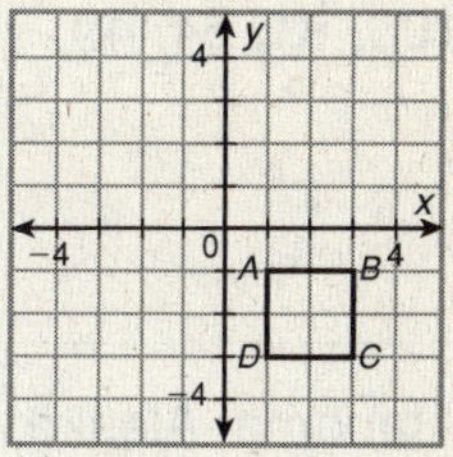

The figure in the plane at right shows the preimage in the transformation $ABCD \rightarrow A'B'C'D'$. Match the number of the image (below) with the name of the correct transformation.

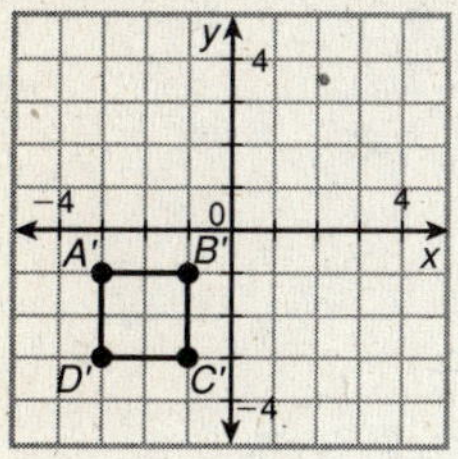

1

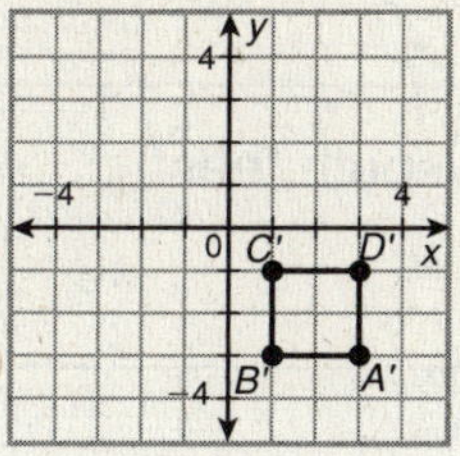

2

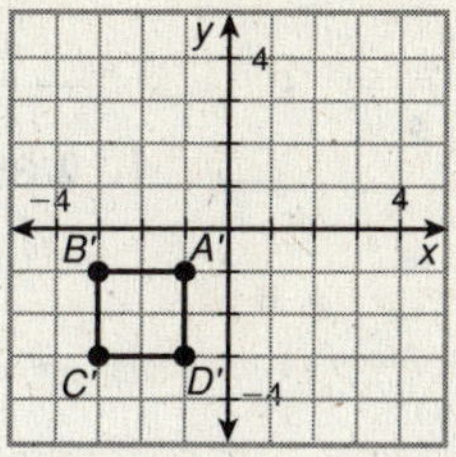

3

1. rotation __________ **2.** translation __________ **3.** reflection __________

4. A figure has vertices at $D(-2, 1)$, $E(-3, 3)$, and $F(0, 3)$. After a transformation, the image of the figure has vertices at $D'(-1, -2)$, $E'(-3, -3)$, and $F'(-3, 0)$. Draw the preimage and the image. Then identify the transformation.

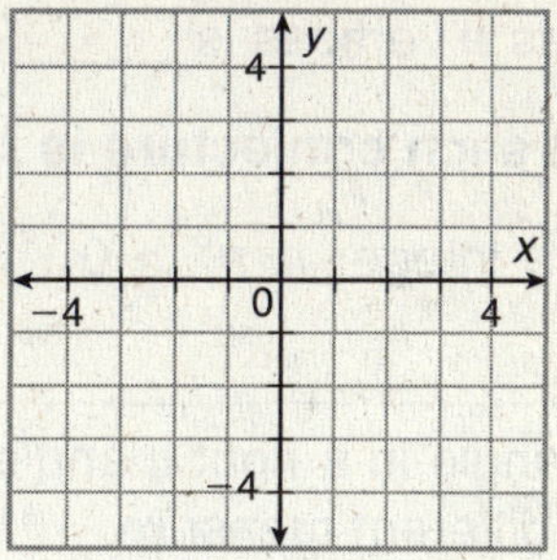

____

5. A figure has vertices at $G(0, 0)$, $H(-1, -2)$, $I(-1.5, 0)$, and $J(-2.5, 2)$. Find the coordinates for the image of $GHIJ$ after the translation $(x, y) \rightarrow (x - 2.5, y + 4)$.

____

Use the figure for Exercise 6.

6. A parking garage attendant will make the most money when the maximum number of cars fits in the parking garage. To fit one more car in, the attendant moves a car from position 1 to position 2. Write a rule for this translation.

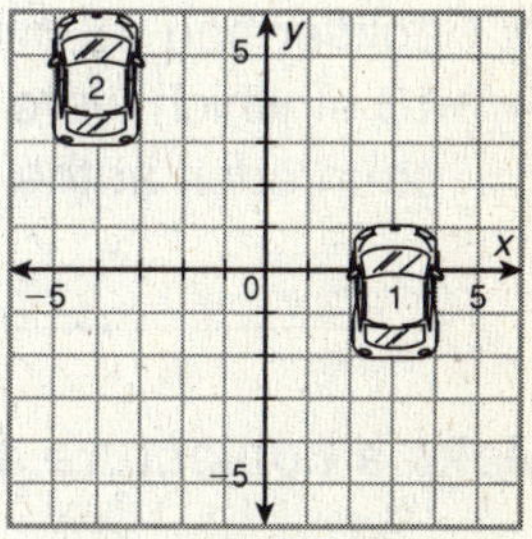

____

7. A figure has vertices at $X(-1, 1)$, $Y(-2, 3)$, and $Z(0, 4)$. Draw the image of XYZ after the translation $(x, y) \rightarrow (x - 2, y)$ and a 180° rotation around X.

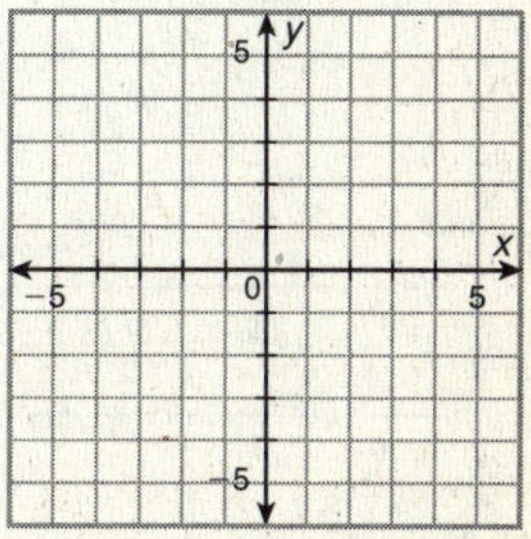

Name ______________________ Date ____________ Class ____________

LESSON 2-1

Practice B

Using Inductive Reasoning to Make Conjectures

Find the next item in each pattern.

1. 100, 81, 64, 49, . . .

____

2.  . . .

____

3. Alabama, Alaska, Arizona, . . .

____

4. west, south, east, . . .

____

Complete each conjecture.

5. The square of any negative number is ______________________.

6. The number of diagonals that can be drawn from one vertex in a convex polygon that has *n* vertices is ______________________.

Show that each conjecture is false by finding a counterexample.

7. For any integer n, $n^3 > 0$.

____

8. Each angle in a right triangle has a different measure.

9. For many years in the United States, each bank printed its own currency. The variety of different bills led to widespread counterfeiting. By the time of the Civil War, a significant fraction of the currency in circulation was counterfeit. If one Civil War soldier had 48 bills, 16 of which were counterfeit, and another soldier had 39 bills, 13 of which were counterfeit, make a conjecture about what fraction of bills were counterfeit at the time of the Civil War.

____

Make a conjecture about each pattern. Write the next two items.

10. 1, 2, 2, 4, 8, 32, . . .

____

____

____

11. 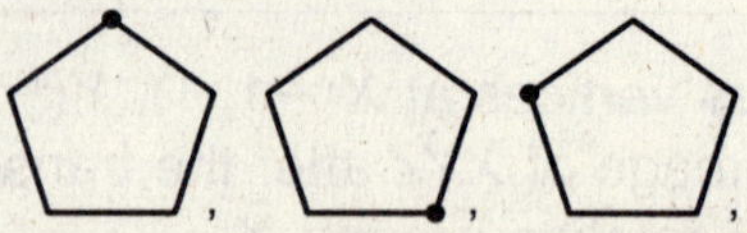 . . .

____

____

Name ______________________________ Date ___________ Class ___________

LESSON 2-2

Practice B

Conditional Statements

Identify the hypothesis and conclusion of each conditional.

1. If you can see the stars, then it is night.

   Hypothesis: ______________________

   Conclusion: ______________________

2. A pencil writes well if it is sharp.

   Hypothesis: ______________________

   Conclusion: ______________________

Write a conditional statement from each of the following.

3. Three noncollinear points determine a plane.

   ____

4. 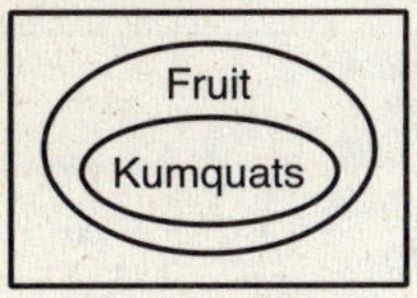

   ____

   ____

   ____

Determine if each conditional is true. If false, give a counterexample.

5. If two points are noncollinear, then a right triangle contains one obtuse angle.

   ____

6. If a liquid is water, then it is composed of hydrogen and oxygen.

   ____

7. If a living thing is green, then it is a plant.

   ____

8. "If *G* is at 4, then *GH* is 3." Write the converse,inverse, and contrapositive of this statement. Find the truth value of each.

   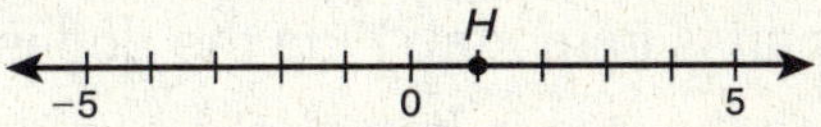

   Converse: ______________________________________

   Inverse: ______________________________________

   Contrapositive: ______________________________________

This chart shows a small part of the *Mammalia* class of animals, the mammals. Write a conditional to describe the relationship between each given pair.

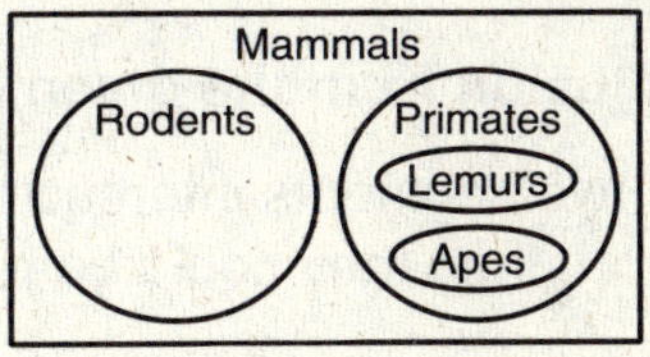

9. primates and mammals ______________________________________

10. lemurs and rodents ______________________________________

11. rodents and apes ______________________________________

12. apes and mammals ______________________________________

Name ______________________________ Date ____________ Class ____________

LESSON 2-3

Practice B

Using Deductive Reasoning to Verify Conjectures

Tell whether each conclusion is a result of inductive or deductive reasoning.

1. The United States Census Bureau collects data on the earnings of American citizens. Using data for the three years from 2001 to 2003, the bureau concluded that the national average median income for a four-person family was $43,527.

____

2. A speeding ticket costs $40 plus $5 per mi/h over the speed limit. Lynne mentions to Frank that she was given a ticket for $75. Frank concludes that Lynne was driving 7 mi/h over the speed limit.

____

Determine if each conjecture is valid by the Law of Detachment.

3. Given: If $m\angle ABC = m\angle CBD$, then $\overrightarrow{BC}$ bisects $\angle ABD$. $\overrightarrow{BC}$ bisects $\angle ABD$.
Conjecture: $m\angle ABC = m\angle CBD$. ____________

4. Given: You will catch a catfish if you use stink bait. Stuart caught a catfish.
Conjecture: Stuart used stink bait. ____________

5. Given: An obtuse triangle has two acute angles. Triangle *ABC* is obtuse.
Conjecture: Triangle *ABC* has two acute angles. ____________

Determine if each conjecture is valid by the Law of Syllogism.

6. Given: If the gossip said it, then it must be true. If it is true, then somebody is in big trouble.
Conjecture: Somebody is in big trouble because the gossip said it. ____________

7. Given: No human is immortal. Fido the dog is not human.
Conjecture: Fido the dog is immortal. ____________

8. Given: The radio is distracting when I am studying. If it is 7:30 P.M. on a weeknight, I am studying.
Conjecture: If it is 7:30 P.M. on a weeknight, the radio is distracting. ____________

Draw a conclusion from the given information.

9. Given: If two segments intersect, then they are not parallel. If two segments are not parallel, then they could be perpendicular. $\overline{EF}$ and $\overline{MN}$ intersect.

____

10. Given: When you are relaxed, your blood pressure is relatively low. If you are sailing, you are relaxed. Becky is sailing.

____

Name ________________________ Date ____________ Class ____________

LESSON 2-4

Practice B

Biconditional Statements and Definitions

Write the conditional statement and converse within each biconditional.

1. The tea kettle is whistling if and only if the water is boiling.

Conditional: ________________________

Converse: ________________________

2. A biconditional is true if and only if the conditional and converse are both true.

Conditional: ________________________

Converse: ________________________

For each conditional, write the converse and a biconditional statement.

3. Conditional: If *n* is an odd number, then $n - 1$ is divisible by 2.

Converse: ________________________

Biconditional: ________________________

4. Conditional: An angle is obtuse when it measures between 90° and 180°.

Converse: ________________________

Biconditional: ________________________

Determine whether a true biconditional can be written from each conditional statement. If not, give a counterexample.

5. If the lamp is unplugged, then the bulb does not shine.

____

6. The date can be the 29th if and only if it is not February.

____

Write each definition as a biconditional.

7. A cube is a three-dimensional solid with six square faces.

____

____

8. Tanya claims that the definition of *doofus* is "her younger brother."

____

____

Name ______________________ Date __________ Class __________

LESSON 2-5

Practice B
Algebraic Proof

Solve each equation. Show all your steps and write a justification for each step.

1. $\frac{1}{5}(a + 10) = -3$

2. $t + 6.5 = 3t - 1.3$

3. The formula for the perimeter P of a rectangle with length ℓ and width w is $P = 2(\ell + w)$. Find the length of the rectangle shown here if the perimeter is $9\frac{1}{2}$ feet. Solve the equation for ℓ and justify each step.

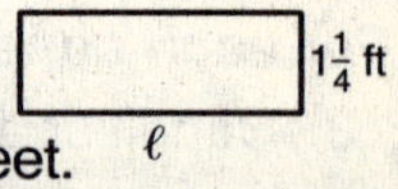

Write a justification for each step.

4.

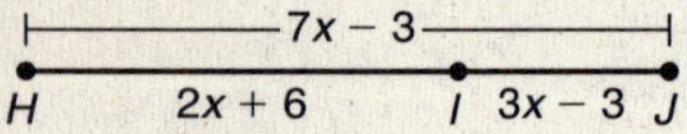

$HJ = HI + IJ$ ______________________

$7x - 3 = (2x + 6) + (3x - 3)$ ______________________

$7x - 3 = 5x + 3$ ______________________

$7x = 5x + 6$ ______________________

$2x = 6$ ______________________

$x = 3$ ______________________

Identify the property that justifies each statement.

5. $m = n$, so $n = m$.

____

6. $\angle ABC \cong \angle ABC$

____

7. $\overline{KL} \cong \overline{LK}$

____

8. $p = q$ and $q = -1$, so $p = -1$.

____

Name ______________________ Date ____________ Class ____________

LESSON 2-6

Practice B
Geometric Proof

Write a justification for each step.

Given: $AB = EF$, B is the midpoint of $\overline{AC}$, and E is the midpoint of $\overline{DF}$.

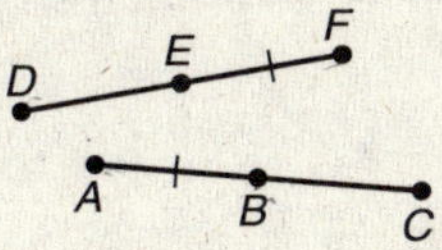

1. B is the midpoint of $\overline{AC}$, and E is the midpoint of $\overline{DF}$. — Given
2. $\overline{AB} \cong \overline{BC}$, and $\overline{DE} \cong \overline{EF}$. — ~~Common seg thrm~~ Def. of midpoint
3. $AB = BC$, and $DE = EF$. — Def. congruent seg.
4. $AB + BC = AC$, and $DE + EF = DF$. — Seg. addition post
5. $2AB = AC$, and $2EF = DF$. — Substitution property
6. $AB = EF$ — Given
7. $2AB = 2EF$ — multiplication property
8. $AC = DF$ — Substitution property
9. $\overline{AC} \cong \overline{DF}$ — ~~Symmetric prop of congruence~~ Def. of congruent segs.

Fill in the blanks to complete the two-column proof.

10. Given: $\angle HKJ$ is a straight angle. $\overrightarrow{KI}$ bisects $\angle HKJ$.

Prove: $\angle IKJ$ is a right angle.

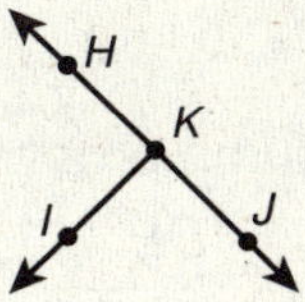

Proof:

Statements	Reasons
1. **a.** ∠HKJ is a straight ∠	1. Given
2. m∠HKJ = 180°	2. **b.** Def. of ~~supplementary~~ straight ∠'s
3. **c.** KI bisects ∠HKJ	3. Given
4. ∠IKJ ≅ ∠IKH	4. Def. of ∠ bisector
5. m∠IKJ = m∠IKH	5. Def. of ≅ ∡s
6. **d.** m∠HJI + m∠JKI = m∠HKJ	6. ∠ Add. Post.
7. 2m∠IKJ = 180°	7. **e.** Subst. (Steps 2, 5, 6)
8. m∠IKJ = 90°	8. Div. Prop. of =
9. ∠IKJ is a right angle.	9. **f.** Def of ⊥ theorem

Name ______________________________ Date ___________ Class ___________

LESSON 2-7

Practice B

Flowchart and Paragraph Proofs

1. Use the given two-column proof to write a flowchart proof.
Given: $\angle 4 \cong \angle 3$
Prove: $m\angle 1 = m\angle 2$

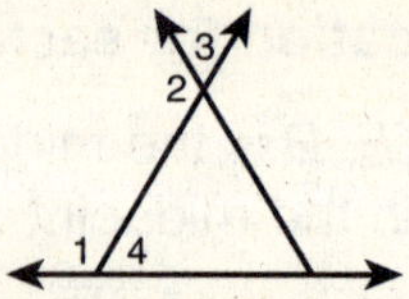

Statements	Reasons
1. $\angle 1$ and $\angle 4$ are supplementary, $\angle 2$ and $\angle 3$ are supplementary.	1. Linear Pair Thm.
2. $\angle 4 \cong \angle 3$	2. Given
3. $\angle 1 \cong \angle 2$	3. $\cong$ Supps. Thm.
4. $m\angle 1 = m\angle 2$	4. Def. of $\cong$ $\angle$s

2. Use the given two-column proof to write a paragraph proof.
Given: $AB = CD$, $BC = DE$
Prove: C is the midpoint of $\overline{AE}$.

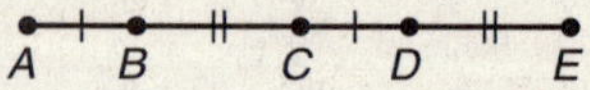

Statements	Reasons
1. $AB = CD$, $BC = DE$	1. Given
2. $AB + BC = CD + DE$	2. Add. Prop. of =
3. $AB + BC = AC$, $CD + DE = CE$	3. Seg. Add. Post.
4. $AC = CE$	4. Subst.
5. $\overline{AC} \cong \overline{CE}$	5. Def. of $\cong$ segs.
6. C is the midpoint of $\overline{AE}$.	6. Def. of mdpt.

____

____

____

____

____

Name ______________________ Date __________ Class __________

LESSON 3-1

Practice B

Lines and Angles

For Exercises 1–4, identify each of the following in the figure.

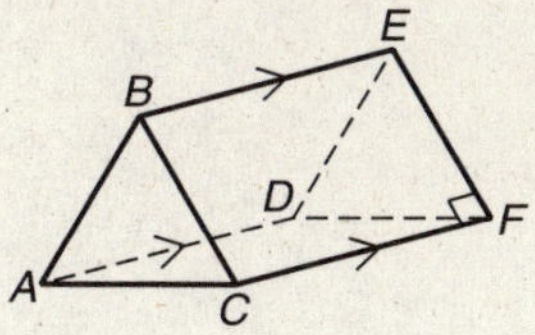

1. a pair of parallel segments ______________________
2. a pair of skew segments ______________________
3. a pair of perpendicular segments ______________________
4. a pair of parallel planes ______________________

In Exercises 5–10, give one example of each from the figure.

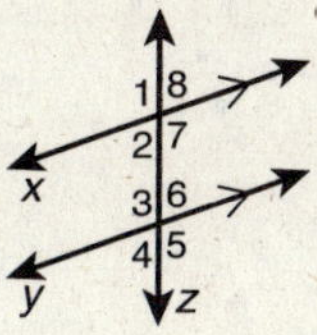

5. a transversal ______________________

6. parallel lines ______________________

7. corresponding angles ______________________

8. alternate interior angles ______________________

9. alternate exterior angles ______________________

10. same-side interior angles ______________________

Use the figure for Exercises 11–14. The figure shows a utility pole with an electrical line and a telephone line. The angled wire is a tension wire. For each angle pair given, identify the transversal and classify the angle pair. (*Hint:* Think of the utility pole as a line for these problems.)

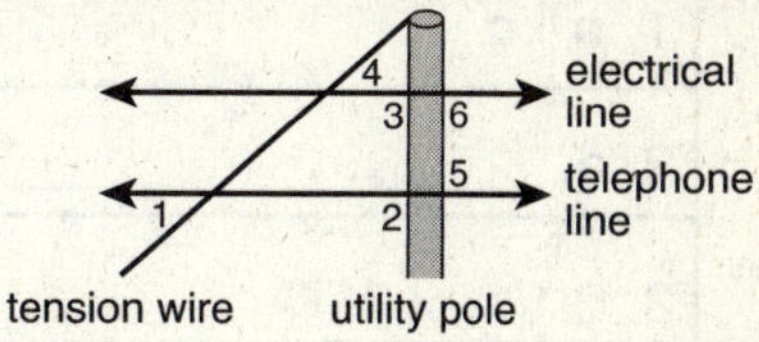

11. ∠5 and ∠6

____

____

12. ∠1 and ∠4

____

____

13. ∠1 and ∠2

____

____

14. ∠5 and ∠3

____

____

Name ______________________ Date __________ Class __________

LESSON 3-2

Practice B
Angles Formed by Parallel Lines and Transversals

Find each angle measure.

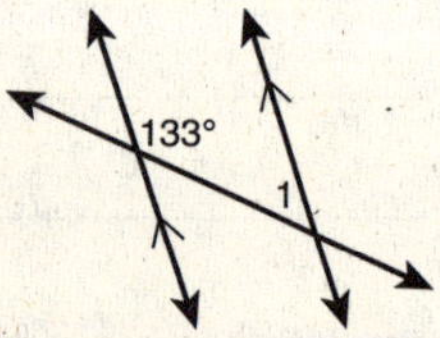

1. m∠1 ____________

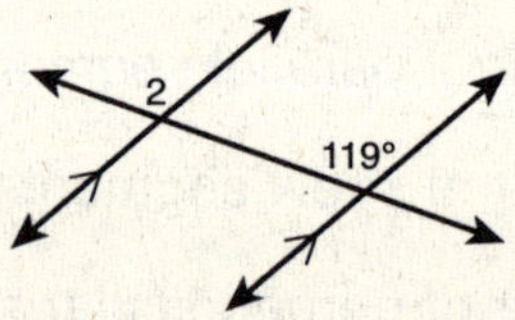

2. m∠2 ____________

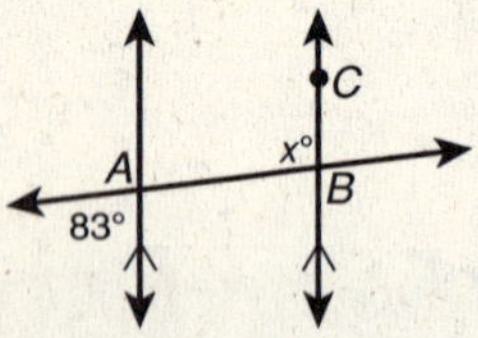

3. m∠*ABC* ____________

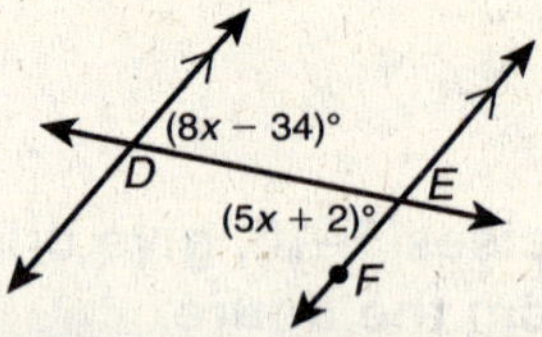

4. m∠*DEF* ____________

Complete the two-column proof to show that same-side exterior angles are supplementary.

5. Given: $p \parallel q$

Prove: $m\angle 1 + m\angle 3 = 180°$

Proof:

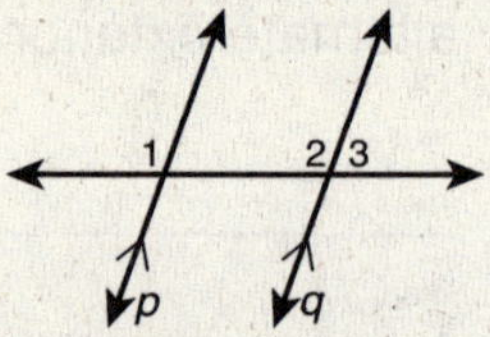

Statements	Reasons
1. $p \parallel q$	1. Given
2. **a.** ____________	2. Lin. Pair Thm.
3. ∠1 ≅ ∠2	3. **b.** ____________
4. **c.** ____________	4. Def. of ≅ ∠s
5. **d.** ____________	5. **e.** ____________

6. Ocean waves move in parallel lines toward the shore. The figure shows Sandy Beaches windsurfing across several waves. For this exercise, think of Sandy's wake as a line. $m\angle 1 = (2x + 2y)°$ and $m\angle 2 = (2x + y)°$. Find x and y.

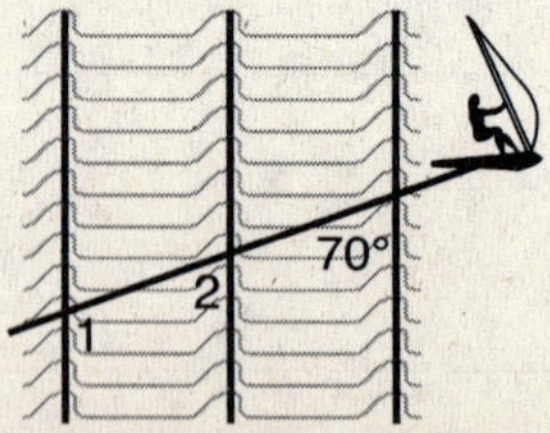

$x =$ ________

$y =$ ________

Name ______________________________ Date ___________ Class ___________

LESSON 3-3

Practice B

Proving Lines Parallel

Use the figure for Exercises 1–8. Tell whether lines *m* and *n* must be parallel from the given information. If they are, state your reasoning. (*Hint:* The angle measures may change for each exercise, and the figure is for reference only.)

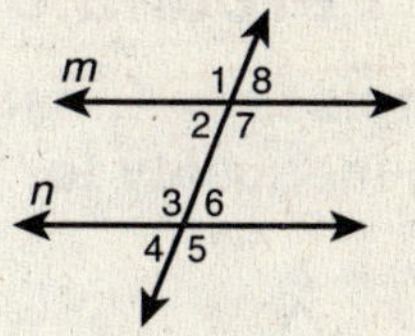

1. $\angle 7 \cong \angle 3$

____

2. $m\angle 3 = (15x + 22)°$, $m\angle 1 = (19x - 10)°$, $x = 8$

____

3. $\angle 7 \cong \angle 6$

____

____

4. $m\angle 2 = (5x + 3)°$, $m\angle 3 = (8x - 5)°$, $x = 14$

____

____

5. $m\angle 8 = (6x - 1)°$, $m\angle 4 = (5x + 3)°$, $x = 9$

____

6. $\angle 5 \cong \angle 7$

____

7. $\angle 1 \cong \angle 5$

____

8. $m\angle 6 = (x + 10)°$, $m\angle 2 = (x + 15)°$

____

9. Look at some of the printed letters in a textbook. The small horizontal and vertical segments attached to the ends of the letters are called *serifs*. Most of the letters in a textbook are in a serif typeface. The letters on this page do not have serifs, so these letters are in a sans-serif typeface. (*Sans* means "without" in French.) The figure shows a capital letter *A* with serifs. Use the given information to write a paragraph proof that the serif, segment $\overline{HI}$, is parallel to segment $\overline{JK}$.

Given: $\angle 1$ and $\angle 3$ are supplementary.

Prove: $\overline{HI} \parallel \overline{JK}$

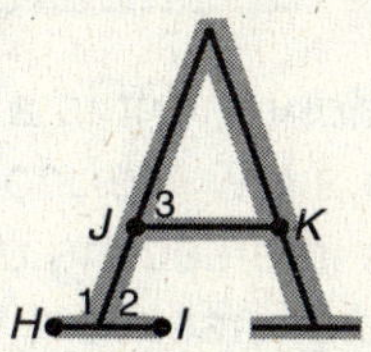

Name ______________________ Date ____________ Class ____________

LESSON 3-4

Practice B

Perpendicular Lines

For Exercises 1–4, name the shortest segment from the point to the line and write an inequality for *x*. (*Hint:* One answer is a double inequality.)

1.

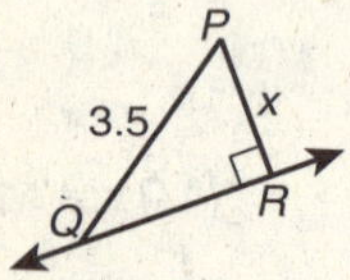

____

2.

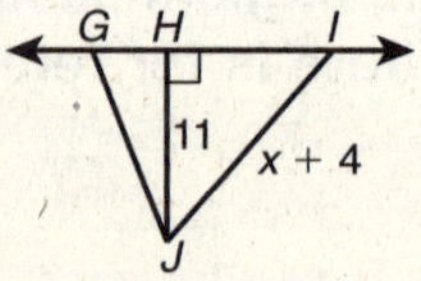

____

3.

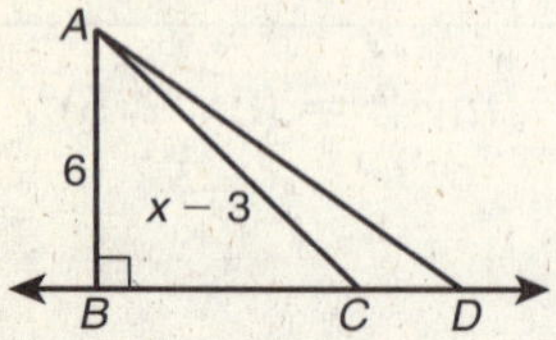

____

4.

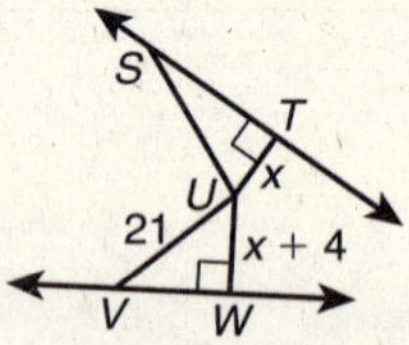

____

Complete the two-column proof.

5. Given: $m \perp n$

Prove: $\angle 1$ and $\angle 2$ are a linear pair of congruent angles.

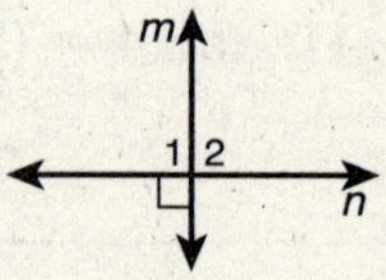

Proof:

Statements	Reasons
1. **a.** ______________	1. Given
2. **b.** ______________	2. Def. of $\perp$
3. $\angle 1 \cong \angle 2$	3. **c.** ______________
4. $m\angle 1 + m\angle 2 = 180°$	4. Add. Prop. of =
5. **d.** ______________	5. Def. of linear pair

6. The Four Corners National Monument is at the intersection of the borders of Arizona, Colorado, New Mexico, and Utah. It is called the four corners because the intersecting borders are perpendicular. If you were to lie down on the intersection, you could be in four states at the same time—the only place in the United States where this is possible. The figure shows the Colorado-Utah border extending north in a straight line until it intersects the Wyoming border at a right angle. Explain why the Colorado-Wyoming border must be parallel to the Colorado–New Mexico border.

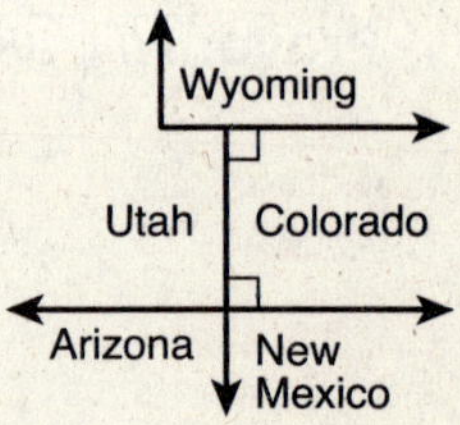

____

____

____

Name ______________________ Date ___________ Class ___________

LESSON 3-5

Practice B
Slopes of Lines

Use the slope formula to determine the slope of each line.

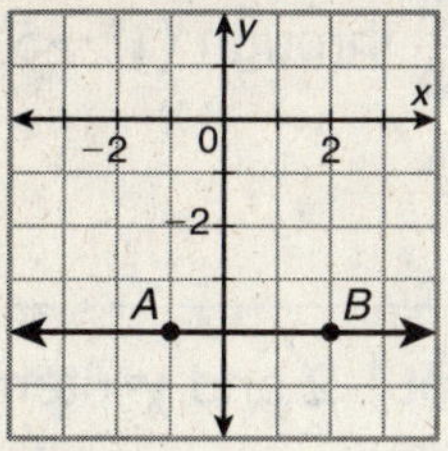

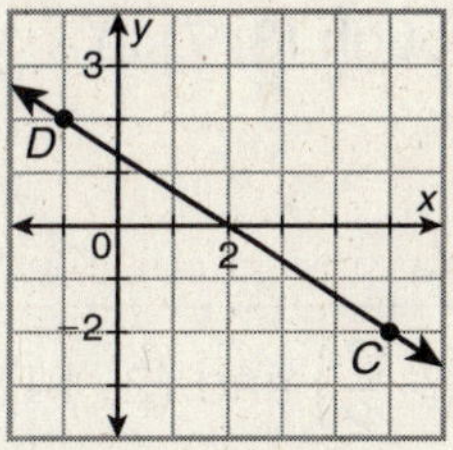

1. $\overleftrightarrow{AB}$ ______________________

2. $\overleftrightarrow{CD}$ ______________________

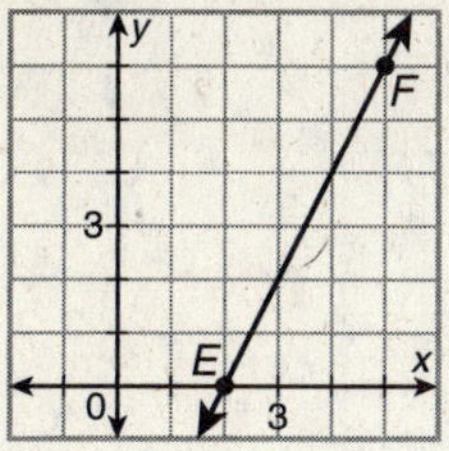

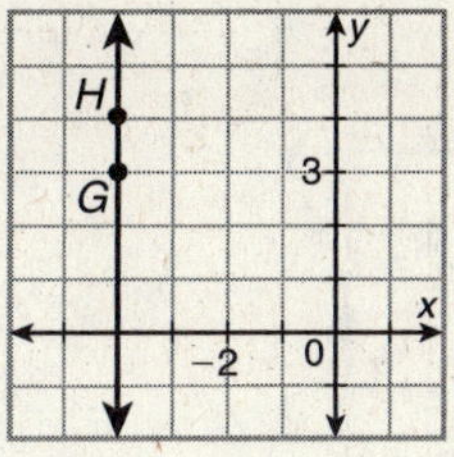

3. $\overleftrightarrow{EF}$ ______________________

4. $\overleftrightarrow{GH}$ ______________________

Graph each pair of lines. Use slopes to determine whether the lines are parallel, perpendicular, or neither.

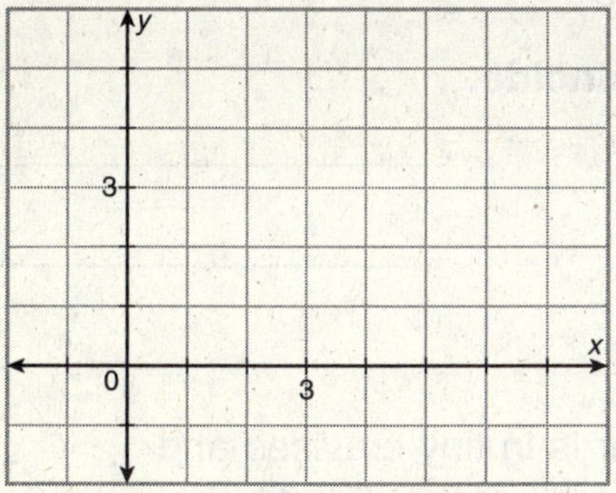

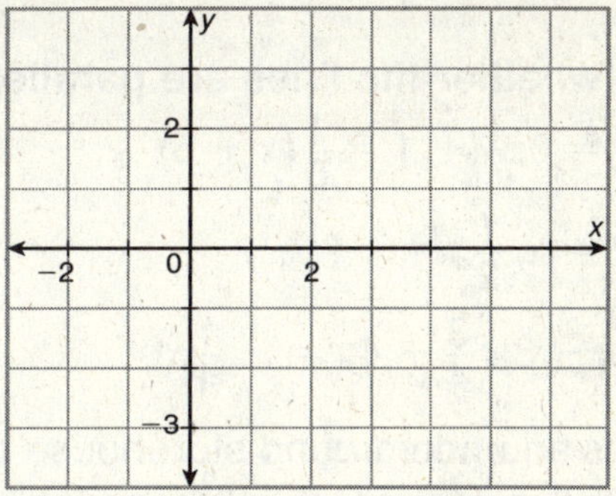

5. $\overleftrightarrow{IJ}$ and $\overleftrightarrow{KL}$ for $I(1, 0)$, $J(5, 3)$, $K(6, -1)$, and $L(0, 2)$ ______________________

6. $\overleftrightarrow{PQ}$ and $\overleftrightarrow{RS}$ for $P(5, 1)$, $Q(-1, -1)$, $R(2, 1)$, and $S(3, -2)$ ______________________

7. At a ski resort, the different ski runs down the mountain are color-coded according to difficulty. Green is easy, blue is medium, and black is hard. Assume that the ski runs below are rated only according to their slope (steeper is harder) and that there is one green, one blue, and one black run. Assign a color to each ski run.

Emerald $\left(m = \frac{4}{7}\right)$ ______________________

Diamond $\left(m = \frac{5}{4}\right)$ ______________________

Ruby $\left(m = \frac{5}{8}\right)$ ______________________

Name ______________________ Date __________ Class __________

LESSON 3-6

Practice B

Lines in the Coordinate Plane

Write the equation of each line in the given form.

1. the horizontal line through (3, 7) in point-slope form

____

2. the line with slope $-\frac{8}{5}$ through (1, −5) in point-slope form

____

3. the line through $\left(-\frac{1}{2}, -\frac{7}{2}\right)$ and (2, 14) in slope-intercept form

____

4. the line with *x*-intercept −2 and *y*-intercept −1 in slope-intercept form

____

Graph each line.

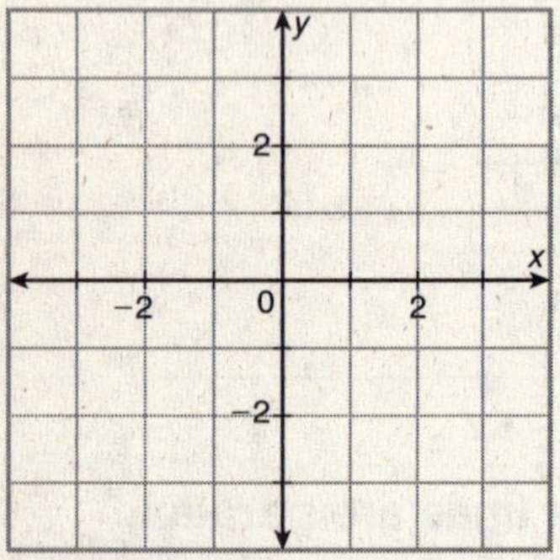

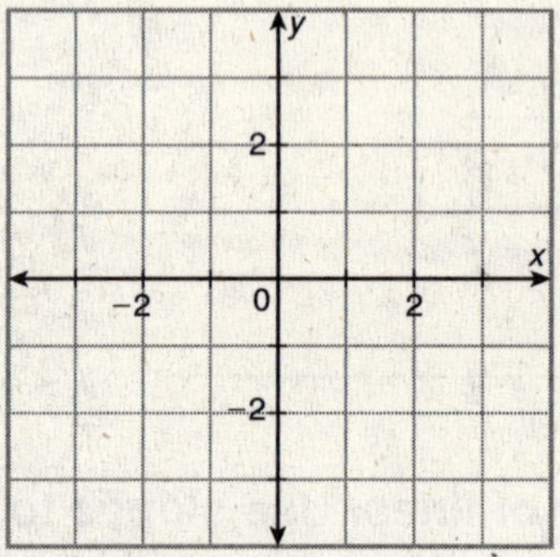

5. $y + 3 = \frac{3}{4}(x + 1)$

6. $y = -\frac{4}{3}x + 2$

Determine whether the lines are parallel, intersect, or coincide.

7. $x - 5y = 0,\ y + 1 = \frac{1}{5}(x + 5)$ _______________

8. $2y + 2 = x,\ \frac{1}{2}x = -1 + y$ _______________

9. $y = 4(x - 3),\ \frac{3}{4} + 4y = -\frac{1}{4}x$ _______________

An *aquifer* is an underground storehouse of water. The water is in tiny crevices and pockets in the rock or sand, but because aquifers underlay large areas of land, the amount of water in an aquifer can be vast. Wells and springs draw water from aquifers.

10. Two relatively small aquifers are the Rush Springs (RS) aquifer and the Arbuckle-Simpson (AS) aquifer, both in Oklahoma. Suppose that starting on a certain day in 1985, 52 million gallons of water per day were taken from the RS aquifer, and 8 million gallons of water per day were taken from the AS aquifer. If the RS aquifer began with 4500 million gallons of water and the AS aquifer began with 3000 million gallons of water and no rain fell, write a slope-intercept equation for each aquifer and find how many days passed until both aquifers held the same amount of water. (Round to the nearest day.)

____

Name ______________________________ Date __________ Class __________

LESSON **4-1**

Practice B

Classifying Triangles

Classify each triangle by its angle measures. (*Note:* Some triangles may belong to more than one class.)

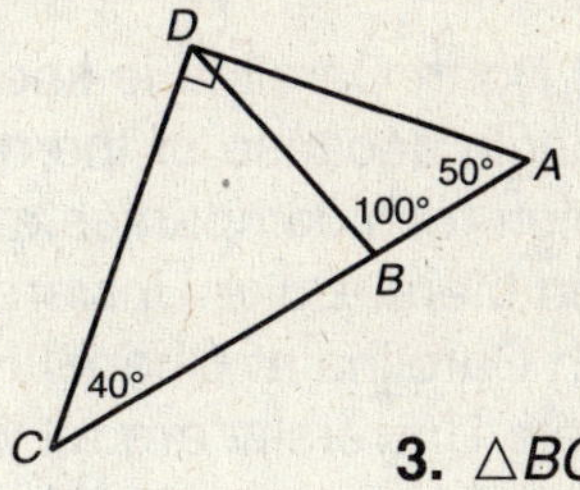

1. $\triangle ABD$ ______________

2. $\triangle ADC$ ______________

3. $\triangle BCD$ ______________

Classify each triangle by its side lengths. (*Note:* Some triangles may belong to more than one class.)

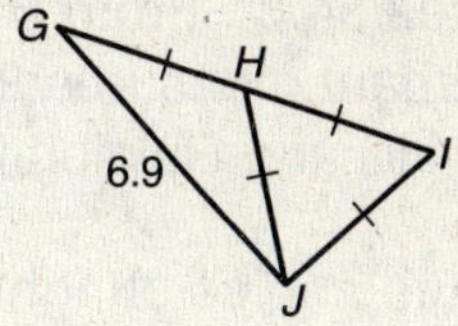

4. $\triangle GIJ$ ______________

5. $\triangle HIJ$ ______________

6. $\triangle GHJ$ ______________

Find the side lengths of each triangle.

7.

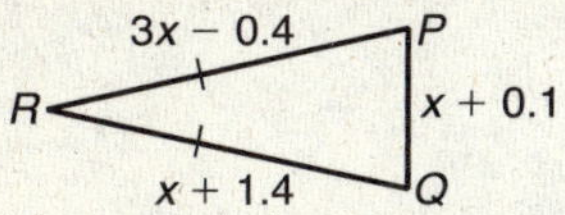

8.

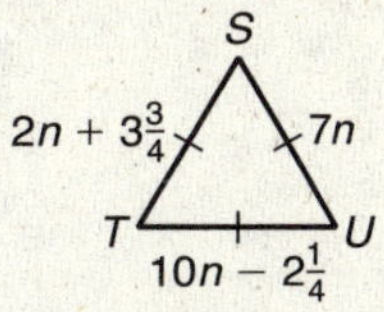

______________ ______________

9. Min works in the kitchen of a catering company. Today her job is to cut whole pita bread into small triangles. Min uses a cutting machine, so every pita triangle comes out the same. The figure shows an example. Min has been told to cut 3 pita triangles for every guest. There will be 250 guests. If the pita bread she uses comes in squares with 20-centimeter sides and she doesn't waste any bread, how many squares of whole pita bread will Min have to cut up?

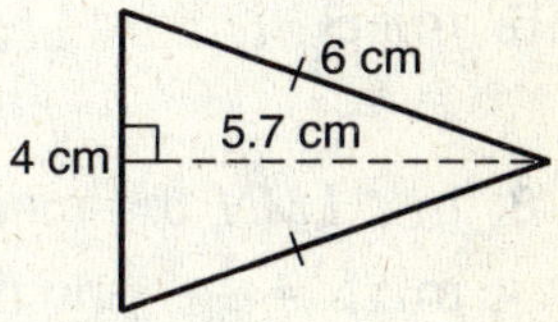

____

10. Follow these instructions and use a protractor to draw a triangle with sides of 3 cm, 4 cm, and 5 cm. First draw a 5-cm segment. Set your compass to 3 cm and make an arc from one end of the 5-cm segment. Now set your compass to 4 cm and make an arc from the other end of the 5-cm segment. Mark the point where the arcs intersect. Connect this point to the ends of the 5-cm segment. Classify the triangle by sides and by angles. Use the Pythagorean Theorem to check your answer.

____

Name ______________________ Date ____________ Class ____________

LESSON 4-2

Practice B

Angle Relationships in Triangles

1. An area in central North Carolina is known as the Research Triangle because of the relatively large number of high-tech companies and research universities located there. Duke University, the University of North Carolina at Chapel Hill, and North Carolina State University are all within this area. The Research Triangle is roughly bounded by the cities of Chapel Hill, Durham, and Raleigh. From Chapel Hill, the angle between Durham and Raleigh measures 54.8°. From Raleigh, the angle between Chapel Hill and Durham measures 24.1°. Find the angle between Chapel Hill and Raleigh from Durham. ____________

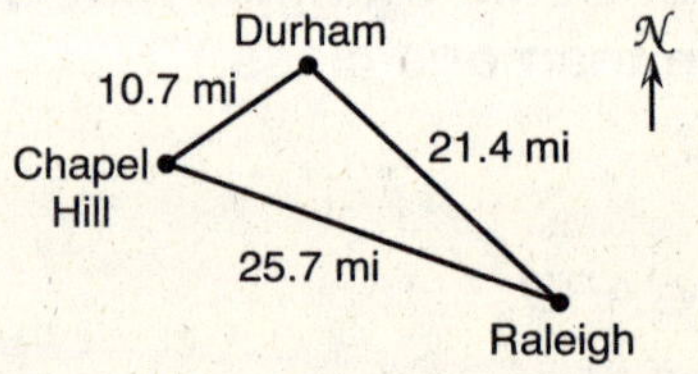

2. The acute angles of right triangle ABC are congruent. Find their measures. ____________

The measure of one of the acute angles in a right triangle is given. Find the measure of the other acute angle.

3. 44.9° ____________   4. $(90 - z)°$ ____________   5. 0.3° ____________

Find each angle measure.

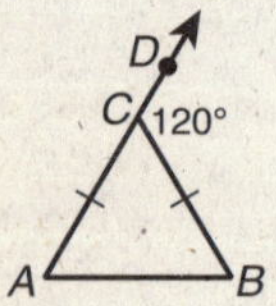

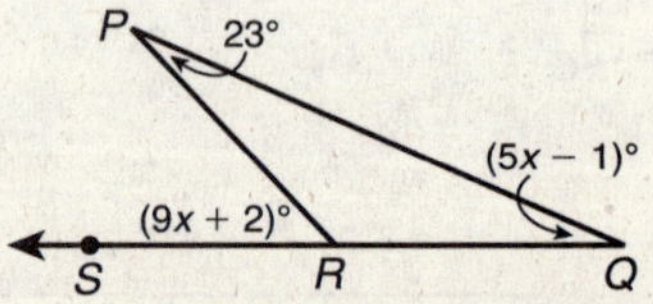

6. m∠B ____________   7. m∠PRS ____________

8. In △LMN, the measure of an exterior angle at N measures 99°. m∠$L = \frac{1}{3}x°$ and m∠$M = \frac{2}{3}x°$. Find m∠L, m∠M, and m∠LNM. ____________

9. m∠E and m∠G ____________   10. m∠T and m∠V ____________

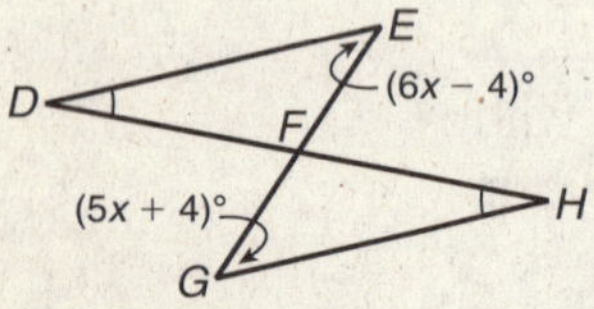

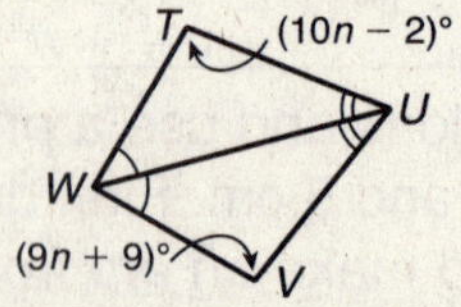

11. In △ABC and △DEF, m∠A = m∠D and m∠B = m∠E. Find m∠F if an exterior angle at A measures 107°, m∠$B = (5x + 2)°$, and m∠$C = (5x + 5)°$. ____________

12. The angle measures of a triangle are in the ratio 3 : 4 : 3. Find the angle measures of the triangle. ____________

Name ____________________ Date __________ Class __________

LESSON 4-5

Practice B

Triangle Congruence: ASA, AAS, and HL

Students in Mrs. Marquez's class are watching a film on the uses of geometry in architecture. The film projector casts the image on a flat screen as shown in the figure. The dotted line is the bisector of $\angle ABC$. Tell whether you can use each congruence theorem to prove that $\triangle ABD \cong \triangle CBD$. If not, tell what else you need to know.

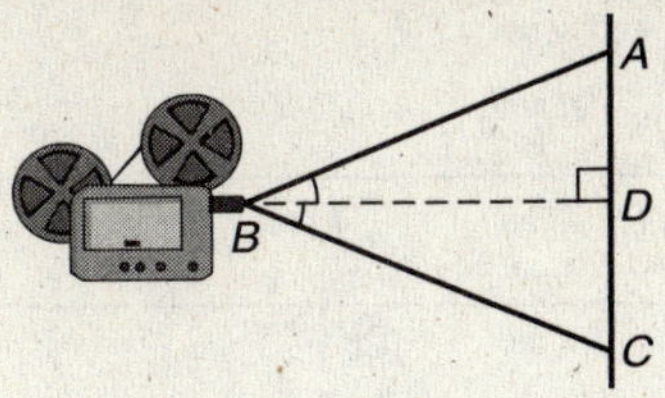

1. Hypotenuse-Leg

____

2. Angle-Side-Angle

____

3. Angle-Angle-Side

____

Write which postulate, if any, can be used to prove the pair of triangles congruent.

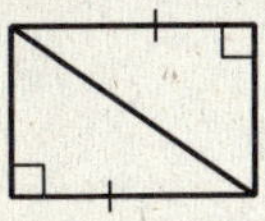

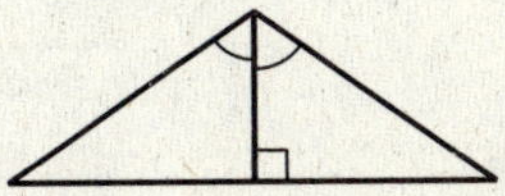

4. ____________________ **5.** ____________________

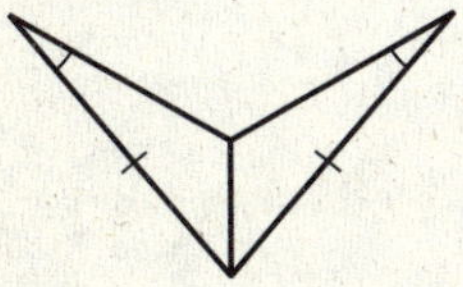

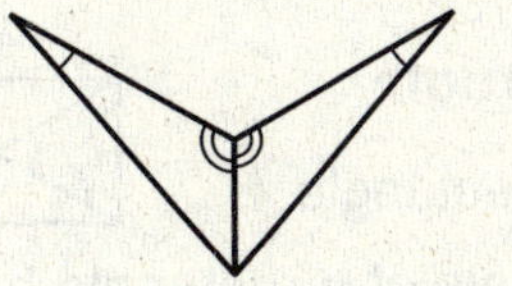

6. ____________________ **7.** ____________________

Write a paragraph proof.

8. Given: $\angle PQU \cong \angle TSU$,
$\angle QUR$ and $\angle SUR$ are right angles.

Prove: $\triangle RUQ \cong \triangle RUS$

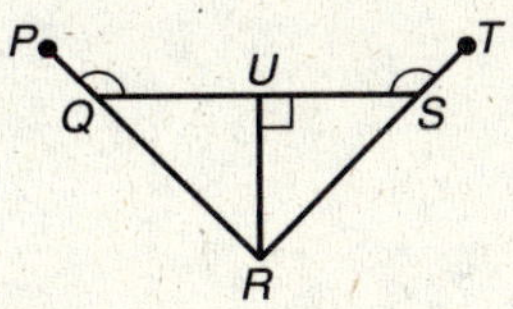

Name ______________________ Date ____________ Class ____________

LESSON 4-6

Practice B

Triangle Congruence: CPCTC

1. Heike Dreschler set the Woman's World Junior Record for the long jump in 1983. She jumped about 23.4 feet. The diagram shows two triangles and a pond. Explain whether Heike could have jumped the pond along path *BA* or along path *CA*.

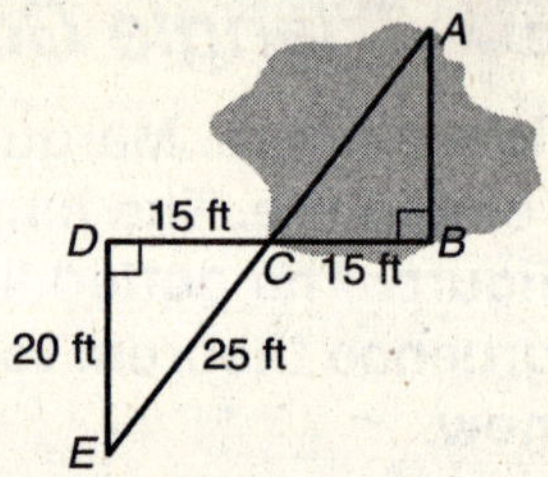

____

____

____

____

____

Write a flowchart proof.

2. **Given:** $\angle L \cong \angle J$, $\overline{KJ} \parallel \overline{LM}$
   Prove: $\angle LKM \cong \angle JMK$

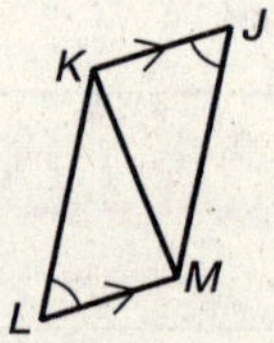

Write a two-column proof.

3. **Given:** *FGHI* is a rectangle.
   Prove: The diagonals of a rectangle have equal lengths.

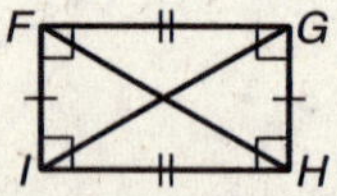

Name ________________________________ Date ____________ Class ____________

LESSON 4-7

Practice B

Introduction to Coordinate Proof

Position an isosceles triangle with sides of 8 units, 5 units, and 5 units in the coordinate plane. Label the coordinates of each vertex. (*Hint:* Use the Pythagorean Theorem.)

1. Center the long side on the *x*-axis at the origin.

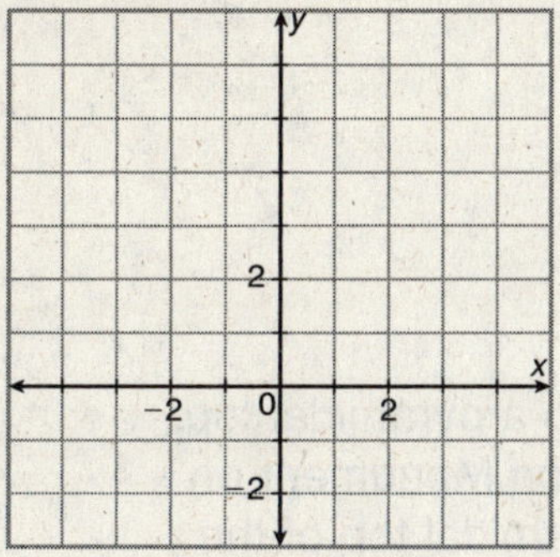

2. Place the long side on the *y*-axis centered at the origin.

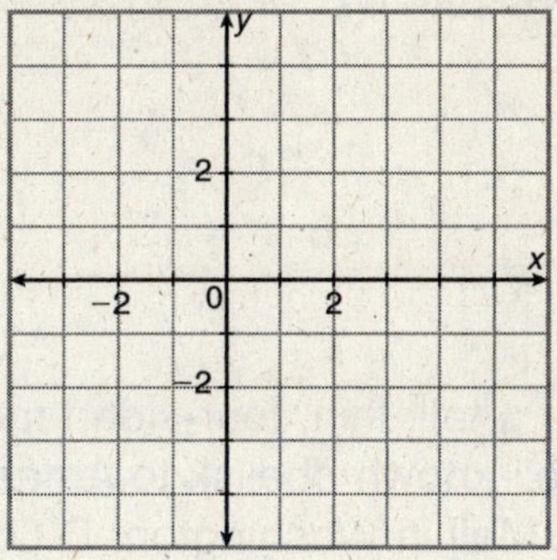

Write a coordinate proof.

3. **Given:** Rectangle *ABCD* has vertices *A*(0, 4), *B*(6, 4), *C*(6, 0), and *D*(0, 0). *E* is the midpoint of $\overline{DC}$. *F* is the midpoint of $\overline{DA}$.

   Prove: The area of rectangle *DEGF* is one-fourth the area of rectangle *ABCD*.

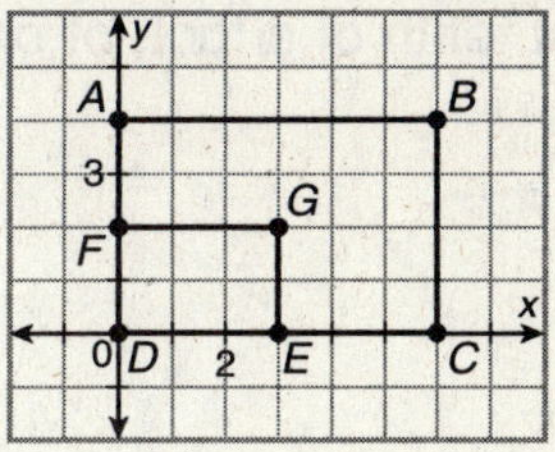

Name ______________________ Date ____________ Class ____________

LESSON 4-8

Practice B

Isosceles and Equilateral Triangles

An altitude of a triangle is a perpendicular segment from a vertex to the line containing the opposite side. Write a paragraph proof that the altitude to the base of an isosceles triangle bisects the base.

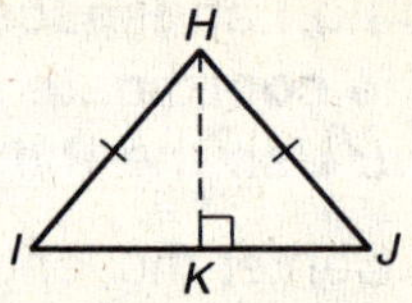

1. Given: $\overline{HI} \cong \overline{HJ}$, $\overline{HK} \perp \overline{IJ}$

Prove: $\overline{HK}$ bisects $\overline{IJ}$.

2. An *obelisk* is a tall, thin, four-sided monument that tapers to a pyramidal top. The most well-known obelisk to Americans is the Washington Monument on the National Mall in Washington, D.C. Each face of the pyramidal top of the Washington Monument is an isosceles triangle. The height of each triangle is 55.5 feet, and the base of each triangle measures 34.4 feet. Find the length, to the nearest tenth of a foot, of one of the two equal legs of the triangle. ____________

Find each value.

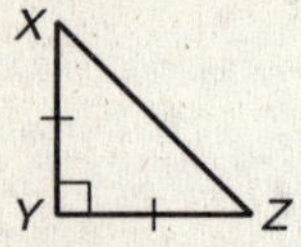

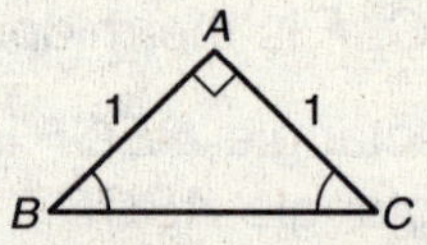

3. m∠X = ____________

4. BC = ____________

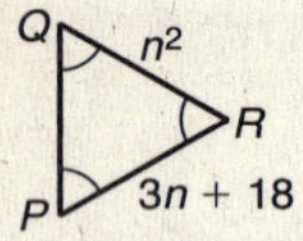

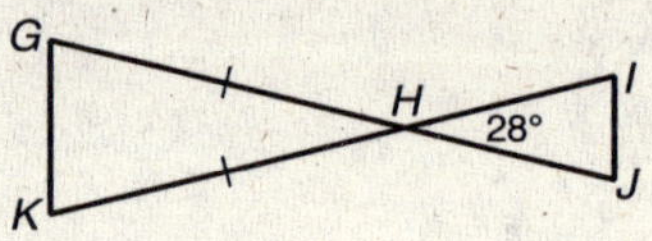

5. PQ = ____________

6. m∠K = ____________

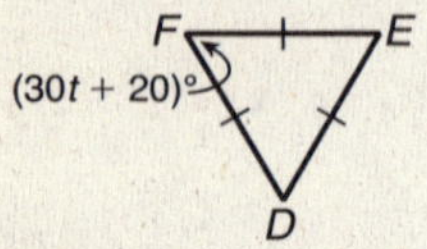

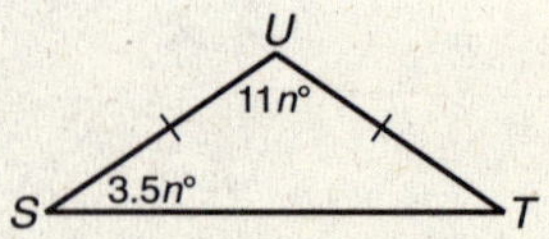

7. t = ____________

8. n = ____________

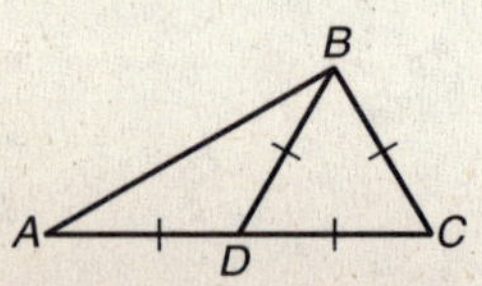

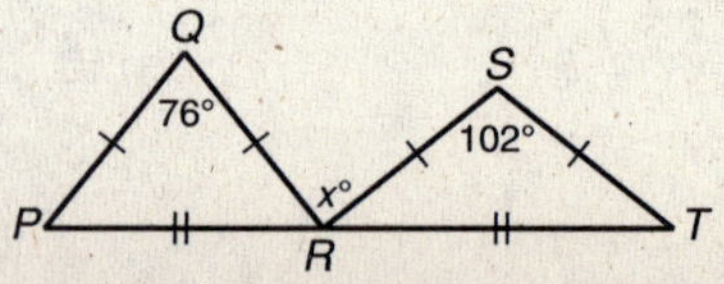

9. m∠A = ____________

10. x = ____________

Name ______________________ Date ____________ Class ____________

LESSON 5-1

Practice B

Perpendicular and Angle Bisectors

Diana is in an archery competition. She stands at *A*, and the target is at *D*. Her competitors stand at *B* and *C*.

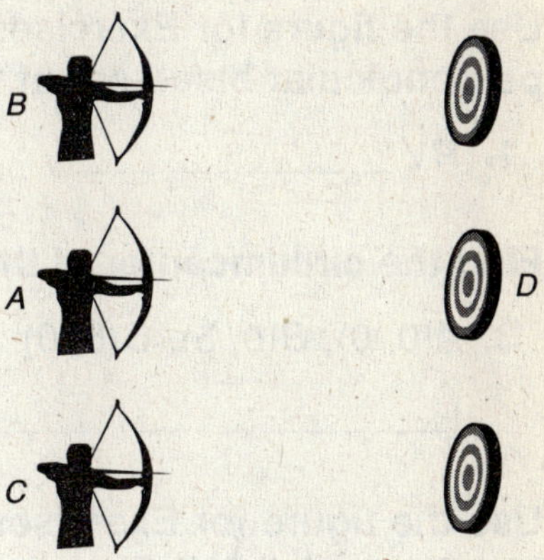

1. The distance from each of her competitors to her target is equal. Explain whether the flight path of Diana's arrow, $\overline{AD}$, must be a perpendicular bisector of $\overline{BC}$.

____

____

____

____

Use the figure for Exercises 2–5.

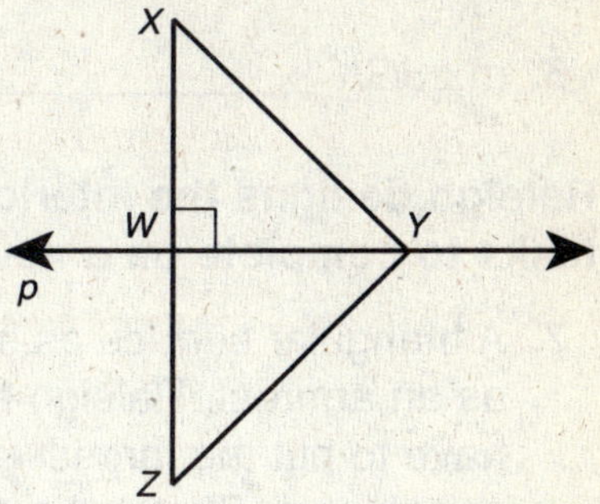

2. Given that line p is the perpendicular bisector of $\overline{XZ}$ and $XY = 15.5$, find ZY. ____________________

3. Given that $XZ = 38$, $YX = 27$, and $YZ = 27$, find ZW. ____________________

4. Given that line p is the perpendicular bisector of $\overline{XZ}$; $XY = 4n$, and $YZ = 14$, find n. ____________________

5. Given that $XY = ZY$, $WX = 6x - 1$, and $XZ = 10x + 16$, find ZW. ____________________

Use the figure for Exercises 6–9.

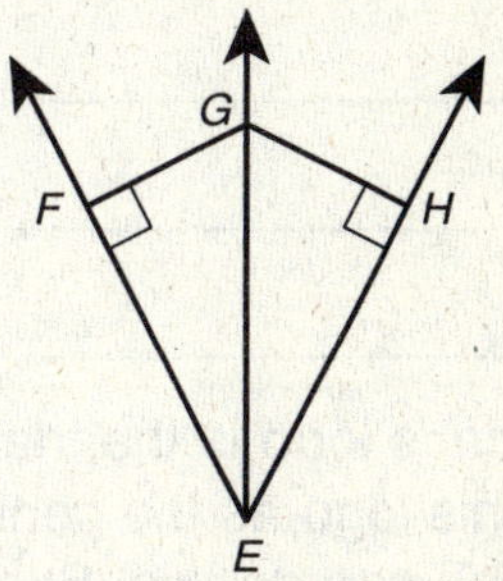

6. Given that $FG = HG$ and $m\angle FEH = 55°$, find $m\angle GEH$. ____________________

7. Given that $\overrightarrow{EG}$ bisects $\angle FEH$ and $GF = \sqrt{2}$, find GH. ____________________

8. Given that $\angle FEG \cong \angle GEH$, $FG = 10z - 30$, and $HG = 7z + 6$, find FG. ____________________

9. Given that $GF = GH$, $m\angle GEF = \frac{8}{3}a°$, and $m\angle GEH = 24°$, find a. ____________________

Write an equation in point-slope form for the perpendicular bisector of the segment with the given endpoints.

10. $L(4, 0)$, $M(-2, 3)$

11. $T(0, -3)$, $U(0, 1)$

12. $A(-1, 6)$, $B(-3, -4)$

____________________ ____________________ ____________________

Name ______________________ Date ____________ Class ____________

LESSON 5-2

Practice B

Bisectors of Triangles

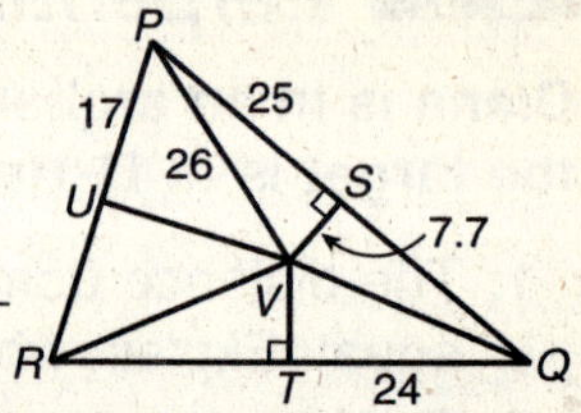

Use the figure for Exercises 1 and 2. $\overline{SV}$, $\overline{TV}$, and $\overline{UV}$ are perpendicular bisectors of the sides of $\triangle PQR$. Find each length.

1. RV ______________

2. TR ______________

Find the circumcenter of the triangle with the given vertices.

3. $A(0, 0)$, $B(0, 5)$, $C(5, 0)$

(______________, ______________)

4. $D(0, 7)$, $E(-3, 1)$, $F(3, 1)$

(______________, ______________)

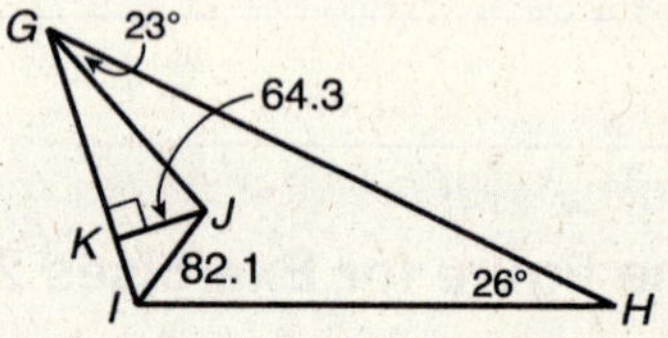

Use the figure for Exercises 7 and 8. $\overline{GJ}$ and $\overline{IJ}$ are angle bisectors of $\triangle GHI$. Find each measure.

5. the distance from J to $\overline{GH}$ ______________

6. $m\angle JGK$ ______________

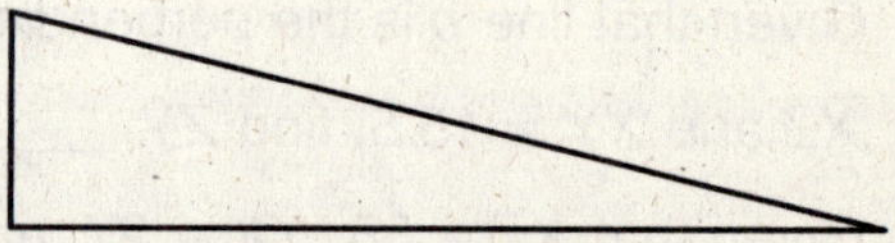

Raleigh designs the interiors of cars. He is given two tasks to complete on a new production model.

7. A triangular surface as shown in the figure is molded into the driver's side door as an armrest. Raleigh thinks he can fit a cup holder into the triangle, but he'll have to put the largest possible circle into the triangle. Explain how Raleigh can do this. Sketch his design on the figure.

____

____

____

____

____

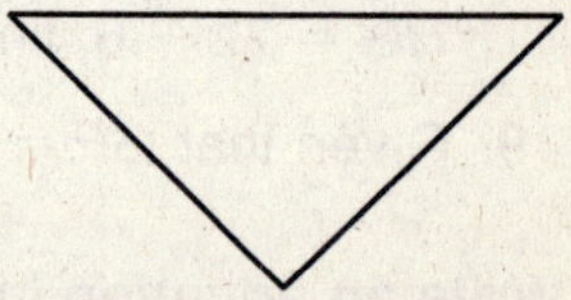

8. The car's logo is the triangle shown in the figure. Raleigh has to use this logo as the center of the steering wheel. Explain how Raleigh can do this. Sketch his design on the figure.

____

____

____

____

____

____

Name ______________________ Date __________ Class __________

LESSON **5-3**

Practice B

Medians and Altitudes of Triangles

Use the figure for Exercises 1–4. $GB = 12\frac{2}{3}$ and $CD = 10$. Find each length.

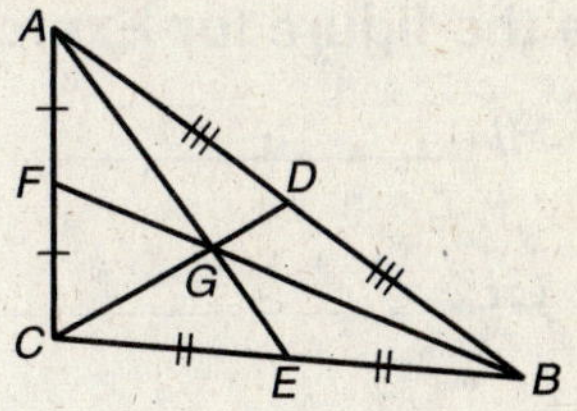

1. *FG* ____________ 2. *BF* ____________

3. *GD* ____________ 4. *CG* ____________

5. A triangular compass needle will turn most easily if it is attached to the compass face through its centroid. Find the coordinates of the centroid.

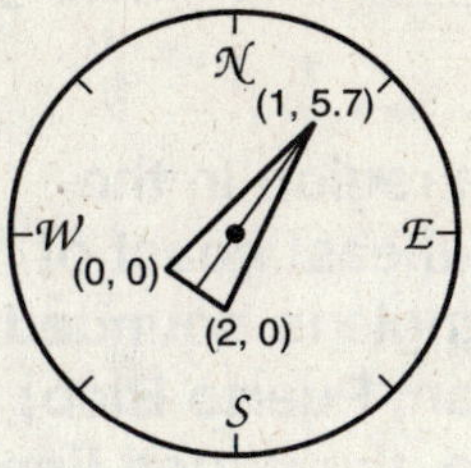

(________, ________)

Find the orthocenter of the triangle with the given vertices.

6. $X(-5, 4)$, $Y(2, -3)$, $Z(1, 4)$ 7. $A(0, -1)$, $B(2, -3)$, $C(4, -1)$

(________, ________) (________, ________)

Use the figure for Exercises 8 and 9. $\overline{HL}$, $\overline{IM}$, and $\overline{JK}$ are medians of $\triangle HIJ$.

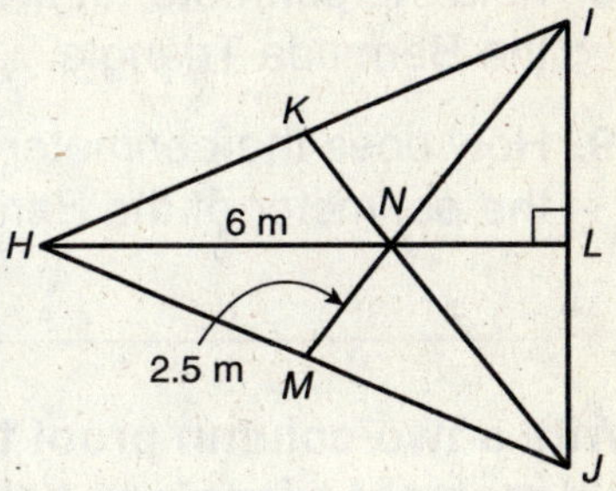

8. Find the area of the triangle. ____________

9. If the perimeter of the triangle is 49 meters, then find the length of $\overline{MH}$. (*Hint:* What kind of a triangle is it?)

____

10. Two medians of a triangle were cut apart at the centroid to make the four segments shown below. Use what you know about the Centroid Theorem to reconstruct the original triangle from the four segments shown. Measure the side lengths of your triangle to check that you constructed medians. (*Note:* There are many possible answers.)

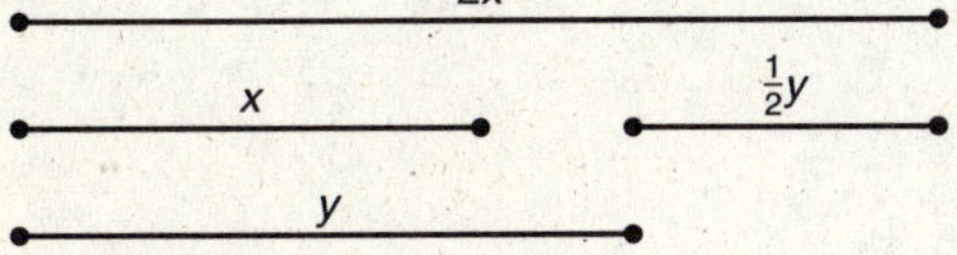

Name ______________________ Date __________ Class __________

LESSON 5-4

Practice B

The Triangle Midsegment Theorem

Use the figure for Exercises 1–6. Find each measure.

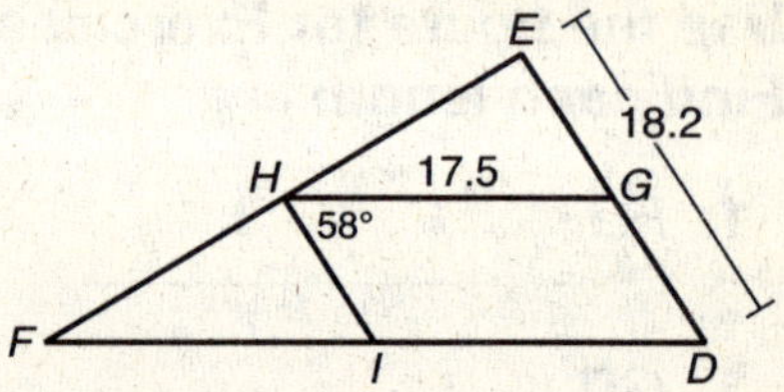

1. HI ______________ 2. DF ______________

3. GE ______________ 4. $m\angle HIF$ ______________

5. $m\angle HGD$ ______________ 6. $m\angle D$ ______________

The Bermuda Triangle is a region in the Atlantic Ocean off the southeast coast of the United States. The triangle is bounded by Miami, Florida; San Juan, Puerto Rico; and Bermuda. In the figure, the dotted lines are midsegments.

	Dist. (mi)
Miami to San Juan	1038
Miami to Bermuda	1042
Bermuda to San Juan	965

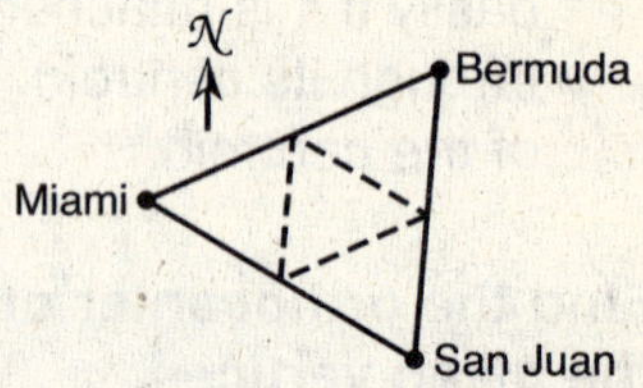

7. Use the distances in the chart to find the perimeter of the Bermuda Triangle. ______________

8. Find the perimeter of the midsegment triangle within the Bermuda Triangle. ______________

9. How does the perimeter of the midsegment triangle compare to the perimeter of the Bermuda Triangle?

____

Write a two-column proof that the perimeter of a midsegment triangle is half the perimeter of the triangle.

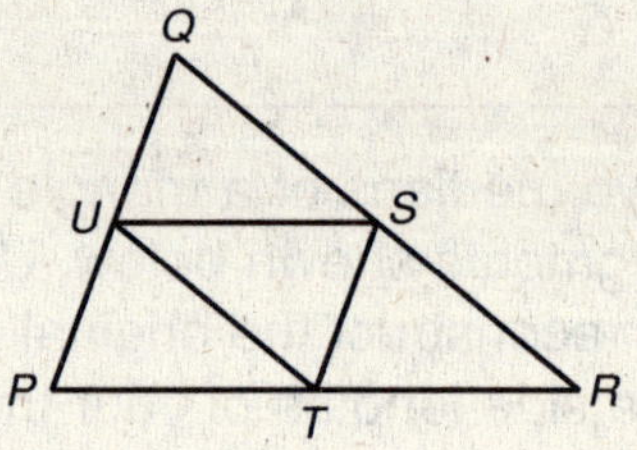

10. **Given:** $\overline{US}$, $\overline{ST}$, and $\overline{TU}$ are midsegments of $\triangle PQR$.

Prove: The perimeter of $\triangle STU = \frac{1}{2}(PQ + QR + RP)$.

Name ______________________________ Date ___________ Class ___________

LESSON 5-5

Practice B

Indirect Proof and Inequalities in One Triangle

Write an indirect proof that the angle measures of a triangle cannot add to more than 180°.

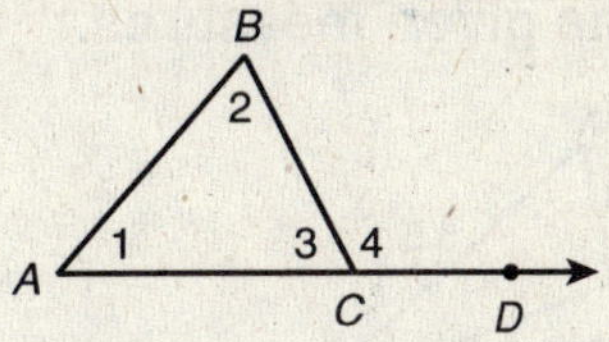

1. State the assumption that starts the indirect proof.

____

2. Use the Exterior Angle Theorem and the Linear Pair Theorem to write the indirect proof.

3. Write the angles of $\triangle DEF$ in order from smallest to largest.

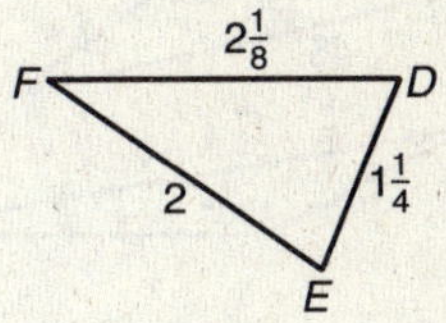

____

4. Write the sides of $\triangle GHI$ in order from shortest to longest.

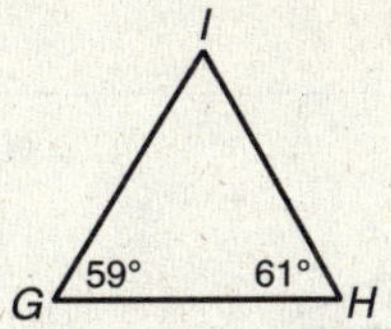

____

Tell whether a triangle can have sides with the given lengths. If not, explain why not.

5. 8, 8, 16 ____________ **6.** 0.5, 0.7, 0.3 ______ **7.** $10\frac{1}{2}$, 4, 14 ______

8. $3x + 2$, x^2, $2x$ when $x = 4$ ______________

9. $3x + 2$, x^2, $2x$ when $x = 6$ ______________

The lengths of two sides of a triangle are given. Find the range of possible lengths for the third side.

10. 8.2 m, 3.5 m **11.** 298 ft, 177 ft **12.** $3\frac{1}{2}$ mi, 4 mi

____________ ____________ ____________

13. The annual Cheese Rolling happens in May at Gloucestershire, England. As the name suggests, large, 7–9 pound wheels of cheese are rolled down a steep hill, and people chase after them. The first person to the bottom wins cheese. Renaldo wants to go to the Cheese Rolling. He plans to leave from Atlanta and fly into London (4281 miles). On the return, he will fly back from London to New York City (3470 miles) to visit his aunt. Then Renaldo heads back to Atlanta. Atlanta, New York City, and London do not lie on the same line. Find the range of the total distance Renaldo could travel on his trip.

____

Name ______________________________ Date ____________ Class ____________

LESSON 5-6

Practice B

Inequalities in Two Triangles

Compare the given measures.

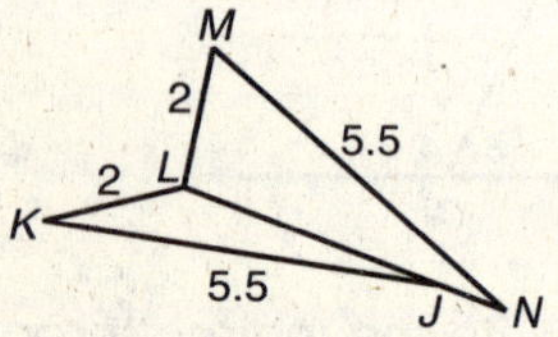

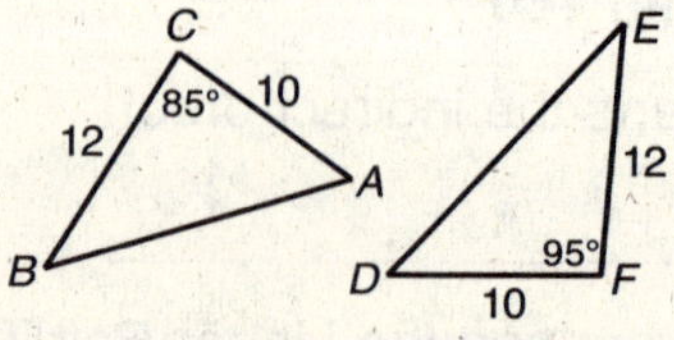

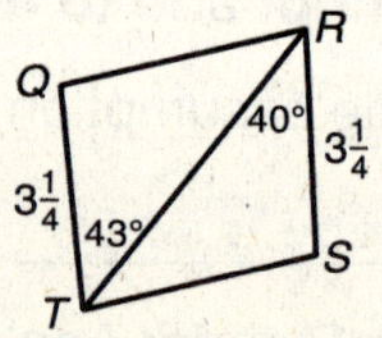

1. m∠K and m∠M ______________

2. AB and DE ______________

3. QR and ST ______________

Find the range of values for *x*.

4.

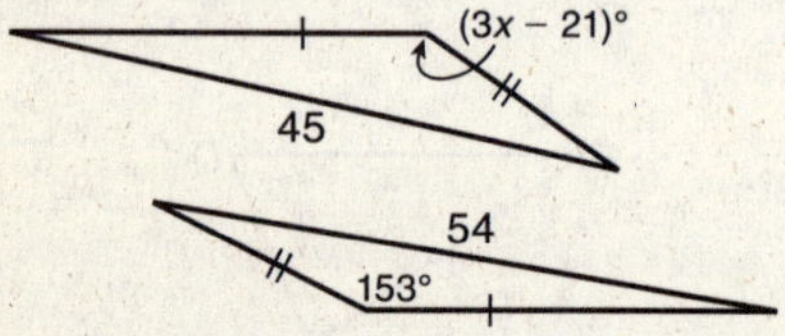

____

6.

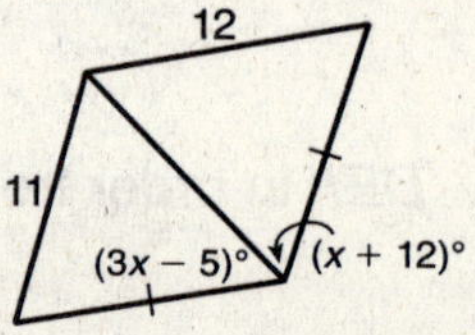

____

5.

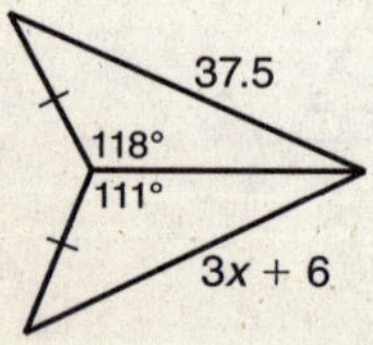

____

7.

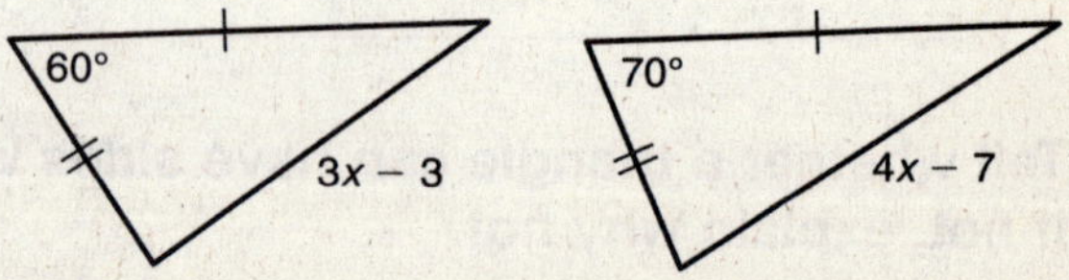

____

8. You have used a compass to copy and bisect segments and angles and to draw arcs and circles. A compass has a drawing leg, a pivot leg, and a hinge at the angle between the legs. Explain why and how the measure of the angle at the hinge changes if you draw two circles with different diameters.

____

____

____

____

____

____

Name ______________________________ Date ____________ Class ____________

LESSON **5-7**

Practice B

The Pythagorean Theorem

Find the value of *x*. Give your answer in simplest radical form.

1.

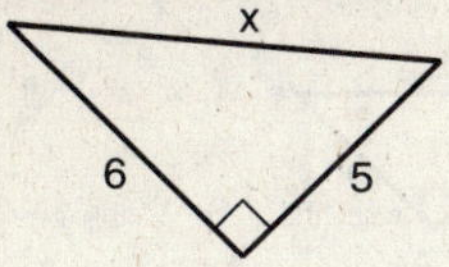

2.

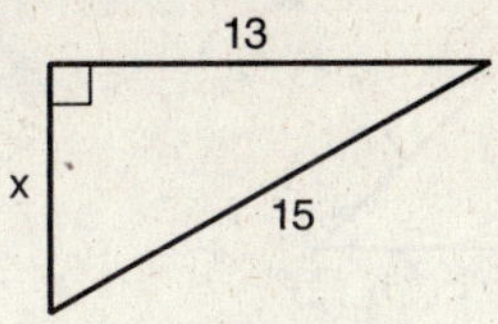

3.

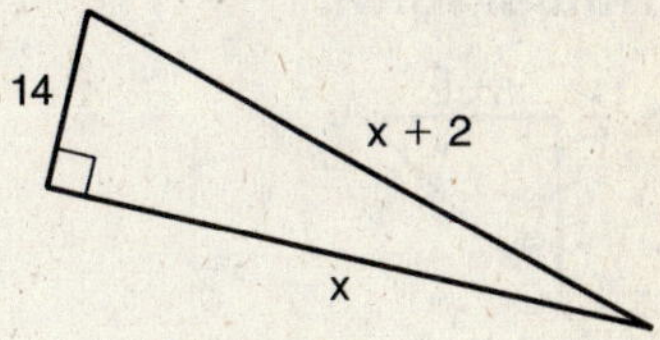

________________ ________________ ________________

4. The aspect ratio of a TV screen is the ratio of the width to the height of the image. A regular TV has an aspect ratio of 4 : 3. Find the height and width of a 42-inch TV screen to the nearest tenth of an inch. (The measure given is the length of the diagonal across the screen.)

____

5. A "wide-screen" TV has an aspect ratio of 16 : 9. Find the length of a diagonal on a wide-screen TV screen that has the same height as the screen in Exercise 4. ________________

Find the missing side lengths. Give your answer in simplest radical form. Tell whether the side lengths form a Pythagorean Triple.

6.

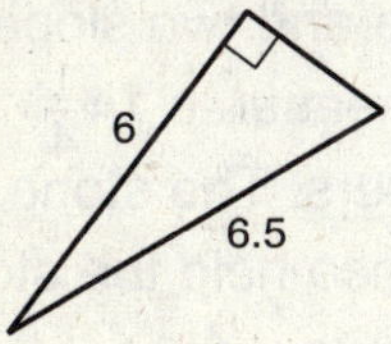

7.

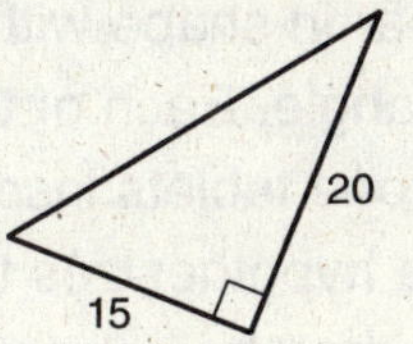

8.

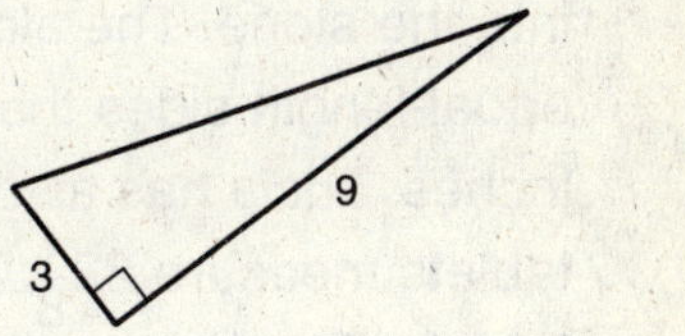

________________ ________________ ________________

Tell whether the measures can be the side lengths of a triangle. If so, classify the triangle as acute, obtuse, or right.

9. 15, 18, 20

10. 7, 8, 11

11. 6, 7, $3\sqrt{13}$

________________ ________________ ________________

12. Kitty has a triangle with sides that measure 16, 8, and 13. She does some calculations and finds that $256 + 64 > 169$. Kitty concludes that the triangle is obtuse. Evaluate Kitty's conclusion and Kitty's reasoning.

____

____

____

____

Name ______________________ Date ____________ Class ____________

LESSON 5-8

Practice B

Applying Special Right Triangles

Find the value of *x* in each figure. Give your answer in simplest radical form.

1.

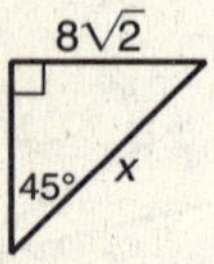

2.

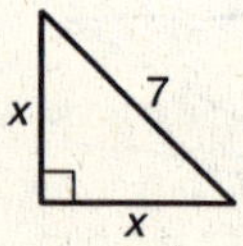

3.

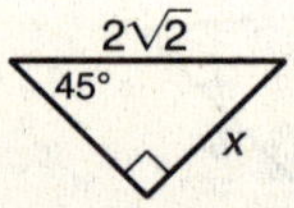

________________ ________________ ________________

Find the values of *x* and *y*. Give your answers in simplest radical form.

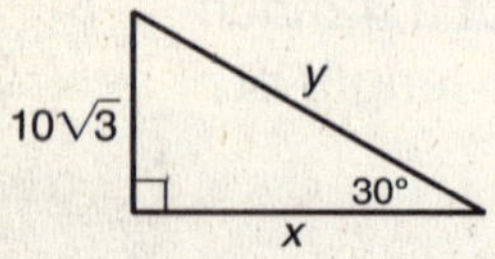

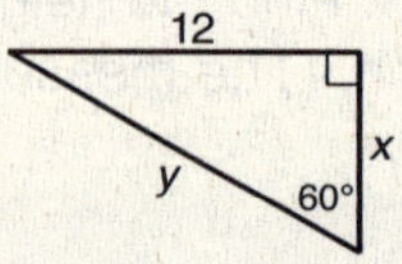

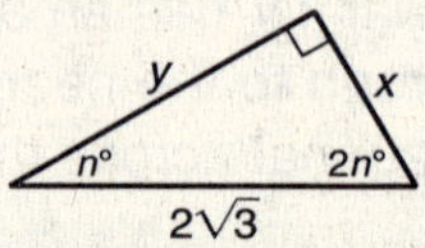

4. $x =$ ________ $y =$ ________ **5.** $x =$ ________ $y =$ ________ **6.** $x =$ ________ $y =$ ________

Lucia is an archaeologist trekking through the jungle of the Yucatan Peninsula. She stumbles upon a stone structure covered with creeper vines and ferns. She immediately begins taking measurements of her discovery. (*Hint:* Drawing some figures may help.)

7. Around the perimeter of the building, Lucia finds small alcoves at regular intervals carved into the stone. The alcoves are triangular in shape with a horizontal base and two sloped equal-length sides that meet at a right angle. Each of the sloped sides measures $14\frac{1}{4}$ inches. Lucia has also found several stone tablets inscribed with characters. The stone tablets measure $22\frac{1}{8}$ inches long. Lucia hypothesizes that the alcoves once held the stone tablets. Tell whether Lucia's hypothesis may be correct. Explain your answer.

____

____

8. Lucia also finds several statues around the building. The statues measure $9\frac{7}{16}$ inches tall. She wonders whether the statues might have been placed in the alcoves. Tell whether this is possible. Explain your answer.

____

____

____

____

____

Name ______________________ Date ____________ Class ____________

LESSON 6-1

Practice B

Properties and Attributes of Polygons

Tell whether each figure is a polygon. If it is a polygon, name it by the number of its sides.

1. 

2. 

3. 

____________ ____________ ____________

4. For a polygon to be regular, it must be both equiangular and equilateral. Name the only type of polygon that must be regular if it is equiangular. ____________

Tell whether each polygon is regular or irregular. Then tell whether it is concave or convex.

5. 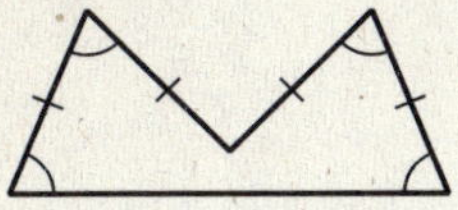

6. 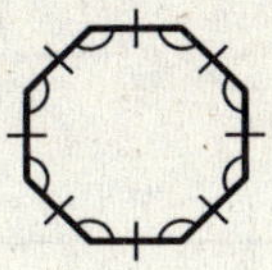

7. 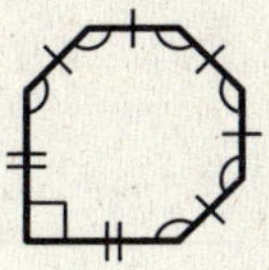

____________ ____________ ____________

8. Find the sum of the interior angle measures of a 14-gon. ____________

9. Find the measure of each interior angle of hexagon *ABCDEF*.

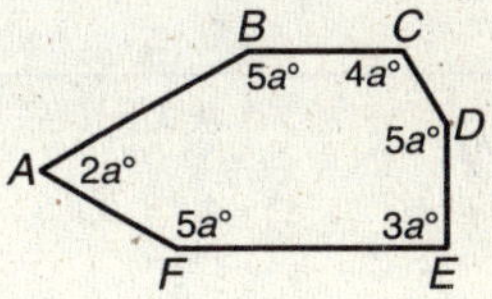

____

____

10. Find the value of n in pentagon *PQRST*.

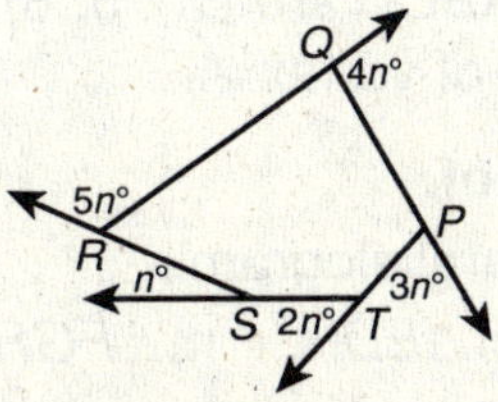

____

Before electric or steam power, a common way to power machinery was with a waterwheel. The simplest form of waterwheel is a series of paddles on a frame partially submerged in a stream. The current in the stream pushes the paddles forward and turns the frame. The power of the turning frame can then be used to drive machinery to saw wood or grind grain. The waterwheel shown has a frame in the shape of a regular octagon.

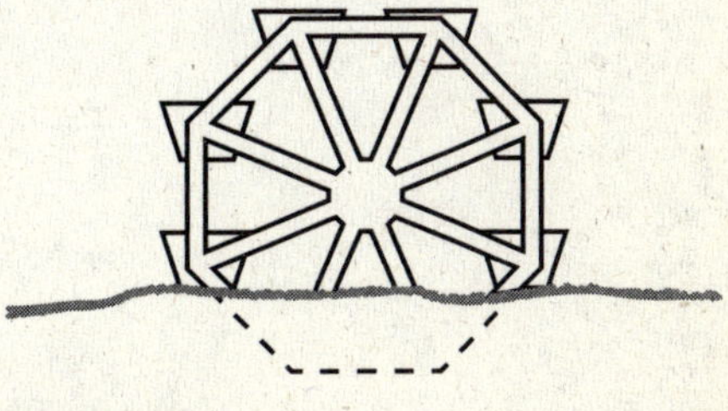

11. Find the measure of one interior angle of the waterwheel. ____________

12. Find the measure of one exterior angle of the waterwheel. ____________

Name ______________________ Date ____________ Class ____________

LESSON 6-2

Practice B

Properties of Parallelograms

A gurney is a wheeled cot or stretcher used in hospitals. Many gurneys are made so that the base will fold up for easy storage in an ambulance. When partially folded, the base forms a parallelogram. In ▱*STUV*, *VU* = 91 centimeters, *UW* = 108.8 centimeters, and m∠*TSV* = 57°. Find each measure.

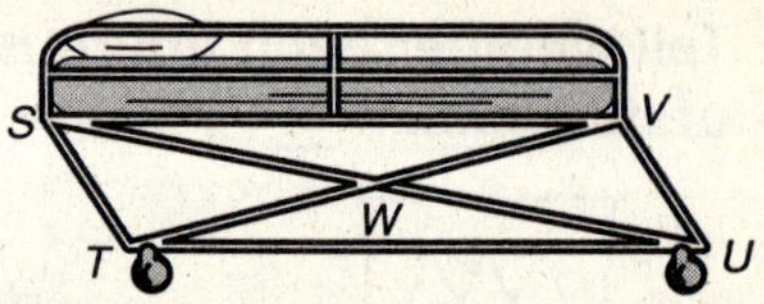

1. *SW* ____________
2. *TS* ____________
3. *US* ____________
4. m∠*SVU* ____________
5. m∠*STU* ____________
6. m∠*TUV* ____________

***JKLM* is a parallelogram. Find each measure.**

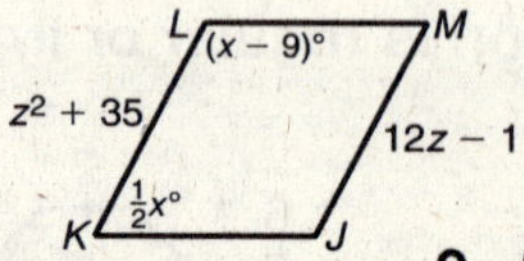

7. m∠*L* ____________
8. m∠*K* ____________
9. *MJ* ____________

***VWXY* is a parallelogram. Find each measure.**

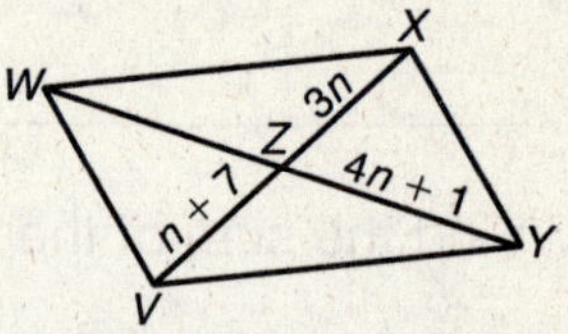

10. *VX* ____________
11. *XZ* ____________
12. *ZW* ____________
13. *WY* ____________

14. Three vertices of ▱*ABCD* are *B*(−3, 3), *C*(2, 7), and *D*(5, 1). Find the coordinates of vertex *A*. ____________

Write a two-column proof.

15. **Given:** *DEFG* is a parallelogram.
    Prove: m∠*DHG* = m∠*EDH* + m∠*FGH*

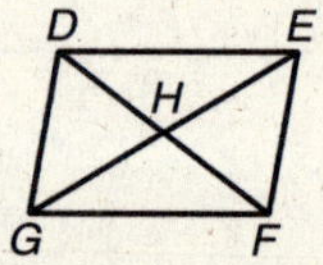

Name ______________________ Date __________ Class __________

LESSON 6-3

Practice B
Conditions for Parallelograms

For Exercises 1 and 2, determine whether the figure is a parallelogram for the given values of the variables. Explain your answers.

1. $x = 9$ and $y = 11$

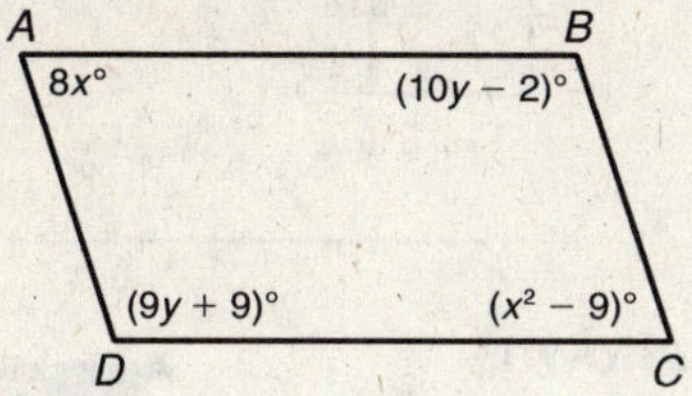

2. $a = 4.3$ and $b = 13$

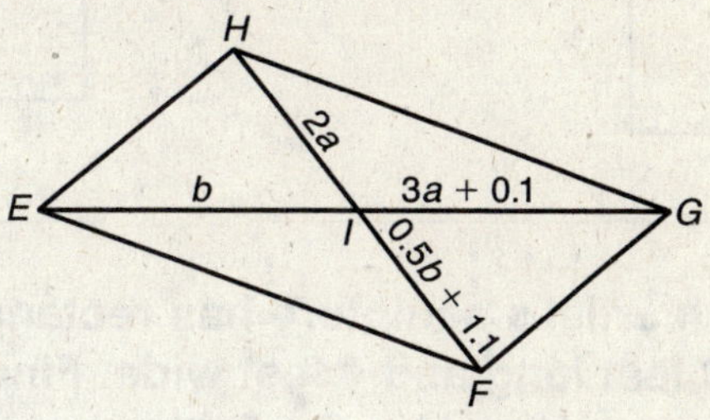

_____________________________ _____________________________

_____________________________ _____________________________

_____________________________ _____________________________

Determine whether each quadrilateral must be a parallelogram. Justify your answers.

3.

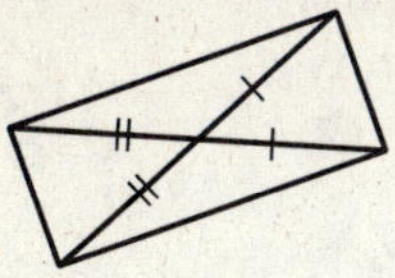

4.

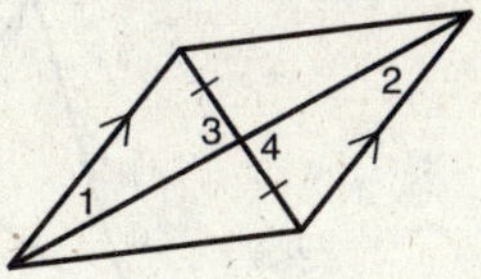

5.

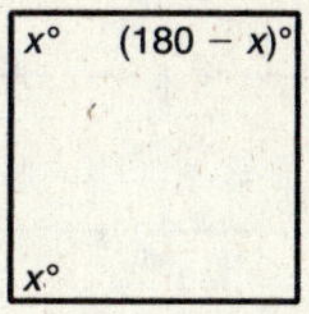

_______________ _______________ _______________

_______________ _______________ _______________

_______________ _______________ _______________

_______________ _______________ _______________

_______________ _______________ _______________

Use the given method to determine whether the quadrilateral with the given vertices is a parallelogram.

6. Find the slopes of all four sides: $J(-4, -1)$, $K(-7, -4)$, $L(2, -10)$, $M(5, -7)$

____

____

7. Find the lengths of all four sides: $P(2, 2)$, $Q(1, -3)$, $R(-4, 2)$, $S(-3, 7)$

____

8. Find the slopes and lengths of one pair of opposite sides:
$T\left(\frac{3}{2}, -2\right)$, $U\left(\frac{3}{2}, 4\right)$, $V\left(-\frac{1}{2}, 0\right)$, $W\left(-\frac{1}{2}, -6\right)$

____

Name ______________________ Date ____________ Class ____________

LESSON 6-4

Practice B

Properties of Special Parallelograms

Tell whether each figure must be a rectangle, rhombus, or square based on the information given. Use the most specific name possible.

1. 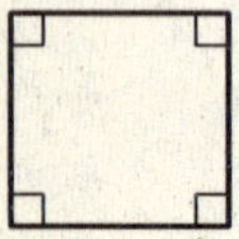

____

2. 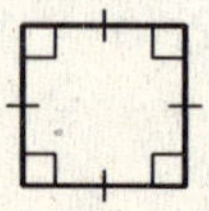

____

3. 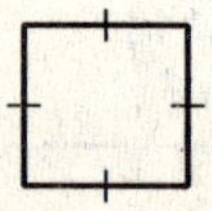

____

A modern artist's sculpture has rectangular faces. The face shown here is 9 feet long and 4 feet wide. Find each measure in simplest radical form. (*Hint:* Use the Pythagorean Theorem.)

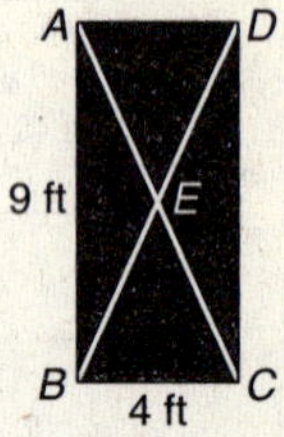

4. DC = ______________________

5. AD = ______________________

6. DB = ______________________

7. AE = ______________________

***VWXY* is a rhombus. Find each measure.**

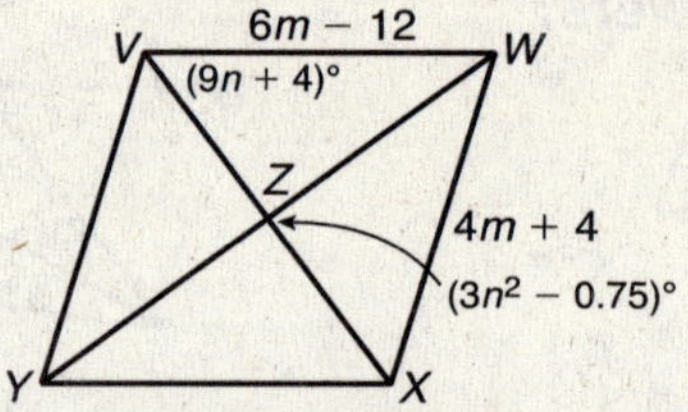

8. XY = ______________________

9. $m\angle YVW$ = ______________________

10. $m\angle VYX$ = ______________________

11. $m\angle XYZ$ = ______________________

12. The vertices of square *JKLM* are $J(-2, 4)$, $K(-3, -1)$, $L(2, -2)$, and $M(3, 3)$. Find each of the following to show that the diagonals of square *JKLM* are congruent perpendicular bisectors of each other.

JL = __________ KM = __________

slope of $\overline{JL}$ = __________ slope of $\overline{KM}$ = __________

midpoint of $\overline{JL}$ = (__________, __________) midpoint of $\overline{KM}$ = (__________, __________)

Write a paragraph proof.

13. Given: *ABCD* is a rectangle.
Prove: $\angle EDC \cong \angle ECD$

Name ________________________________ Date __________ Class __________

LESSON 6-5

Practice B

Conditions for Special Parallelograms

1. On the National Mall in Washington, D.C., a reflecting pool lies between the Lincoln Memorial and the World War II Memorial. The pool has two 2300-foot-long sides and two 150-foot-long sides. Tell what additional information you need to know in order to determine whether the reflecting pool is a rectangle. (*Hint:* Remember that you have to show it is a parallelogram first.)

____

____

____

____

Use the figure for Exercises 2–5. Determine whether each conclusion is valid. If not, tell what additional information is needed to make it valid.

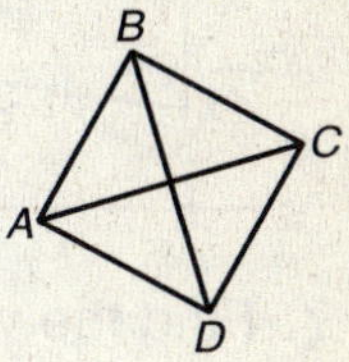

2. **Given:** $\overline{AC}$ and $\overline{BD}$ bisect each other. $\overline{AC} \cong \overline{BD}$
   Conclusion: *ABCD* is a square.

____

3. **Given:** $\overline{AC} \perp \overline{BD}$, $\overline{AB} \cong \overline{BC}$
   Conclusion: *ABCD* is a rhombus.

____

4. **Given:** $\overline{AB} \cong \overline{DC}$, $\overline{AD} \cong \overline{BC}$, $m\angle ADB = m\angle ABD = 45°$
   Conclusion: *ABCD* is a square.

____

5. **Given:** $\overline{AB} \parallel \overline{DC}$, $\overline{AD} \cong \overline{BC}$, $\overline{AC} \cong \overline{BD}$
   Conclusion: *ABCD* is a rectangle.

____

Find the lengths and slopes of the diagonals to determine whether a parallelogram with the given vertices is a rectangle, rhombus, or square. Give all names that apply.

6. $E(-2, -4)$, $F(0, -1)$, $G(-3, 1)$, $H(-5, -2)$ ____________________

   EG = __________ FH = __________

   slope of $\overline{EG}$ = __________ slope of $\overline{FH}$ = __________

7. $P(-1, 3)$, $Q(-2, 5)$, $R(0, 4)$, $S(1, 2)$ ____________________

   PR = __________ QS = __________

   slope of $\overline{PR}$ = __________ slope of $\overline{QS}$ = __________

Name ______________________ Date ____________ Class ____________

LESSON 6-6

Practice B

Properties of Kites and Trapezoids

In kite *ABCD*, m∠*BAC* = 35° and m∠*BCD* = 44°. For Exercises 1–3, find each measure.

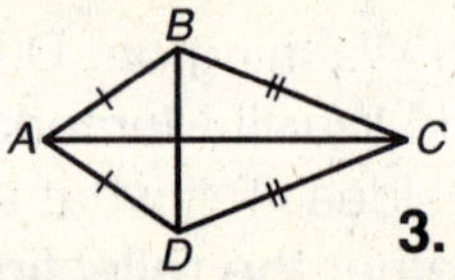

1. m∠*ABD* ____________
2. m∠*DCA* ____________
3. m∠*ABC* ____________

4. Find the area of △*EFG*. ____________

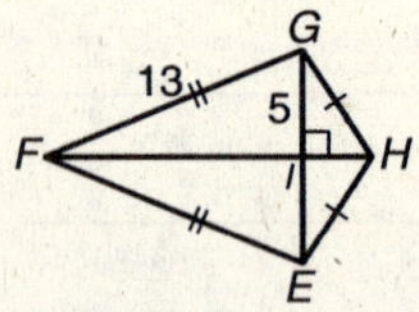

5. Find m∠*Z*.

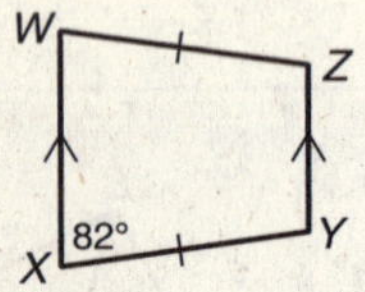

____

6. *KM* = 7.5, and *NM* = 2.6. Find *LN*.

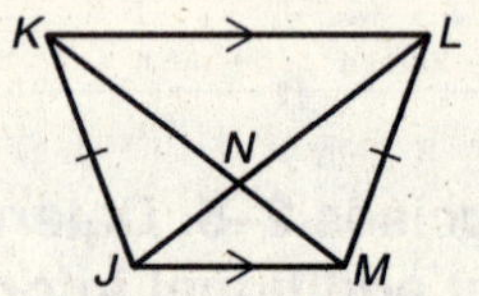

____

7. Find the value of *n* so that *PQRS* is isosceles.

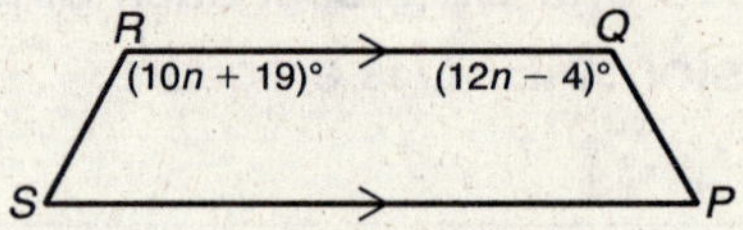

____

8. Find the value of *x* so that *EFGH* is isosceles.

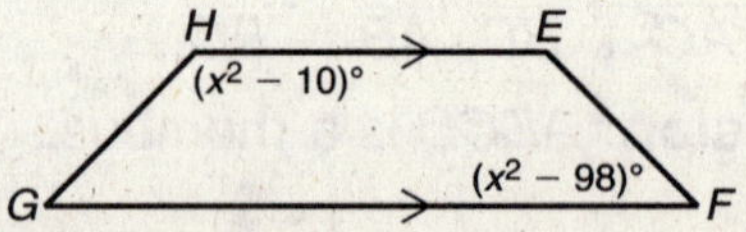

____

9. *BD* = 7*a* − 0.5, and *AC* = 5*a* + 2.3. Find the value of *a* so that *ABCD* is isosceles.

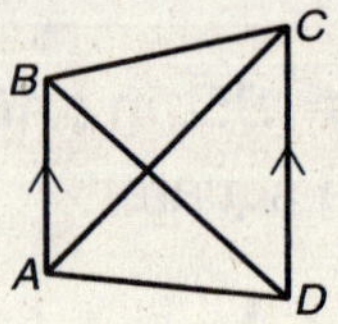

____

10. *QS* = $8z^2$, and *RT* = $6z^2 + 38$. Find the value of *z* so that *QRST* is isosceles.

____

Use the figure for Exercises 11 and 12. The figure shows a *ziggurat*. A ziggurat is a stepped, flat-topped pyramid that was used as a temple by ancient peoples of Mesopotamia. The dashed lines show that a ziggurat has sides roughly in the shape of a trapezoid.

11. Each "step" in the ziggurat has equal height. Give the vocabulary term for $\overline{MN}$.

____

12. The bottom of the ziggurat is 27.3 meters long, and the top of the ziggurat is 11.6 meters long. Find *MN*.

____

Name ______________________ Date __________ Class __________

LESSON 7-1

Practice B

Ratio and Proportion

Use the graph for Exercises 1–3. Write a ratio expressing the slope of each line.

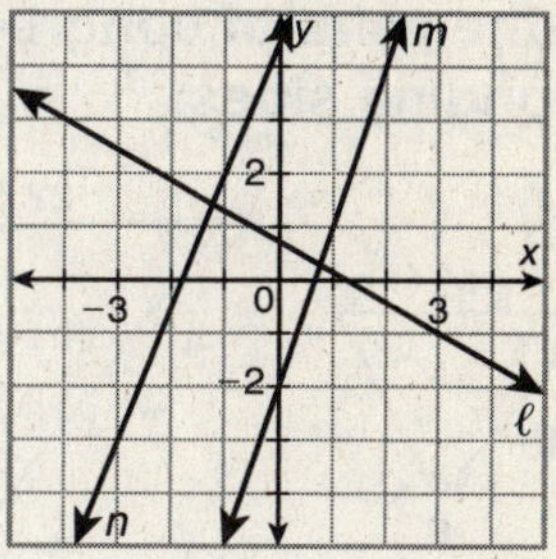

1. ℓ ______________

2. m ______________

3. n ______________

4. The ratio of the angle measures in a quadrilateral is 1 : 4 : 5 : 6. Find each angle measure. ______________

5. The ratio of the side lengths in a rectangle is 5 : 2 : 5 : 2, and its area is 90 square feet. Find the side lengths. ______________

For part of her homework, Celia measured the angles and the lengths of the sides of two triangles. She wrote down the ratios for angle measures and side lengths. Two of the ratios were 4 : 7 : 8 and 3 : 8 : 13.

6. When Celia got to school the next day, she couldn't remember which ratio was for angles and which was for sides. Tell which must be the ratio of the lengths of the sides. Explain your answer.

____

____

____

____

7. Find the measures of the angles of one of Celia's triangles. ______________

Solve each proportion.

8. $\frac{28}{p} = \frac{42}{3}$

$p =$ ______________

9. $\frac{28}{24} = \frac{q}{102}$

$q =$ ______________

10. $\frac{3}{4.5} = \frac{7}{r}$

$r =$ ______________

11. $\frac{9}{s} = \frac{s}{25}$

$s =$ ______________

12. $\frac{50}{2t + 4} = \frac{2t + 4}{2}$

$t =$ ______________

13. $\frac{u + 3}{8} = \frac{5}{u - 3}$

$u =$ ______________

14. Given that $12a = 20b$, find the ratio of a to b in simplest form. ______________

15. Given that $34x = 51y$, find the ratio $x : y$ in simplest form. ______________

Name ______________________ Date ____________ Class ____________

LESSON 7-2

Practice B

Ratios in Similar Polygons

Identify the pairs of congruent corresponding angles and the corresponding sides.

1.

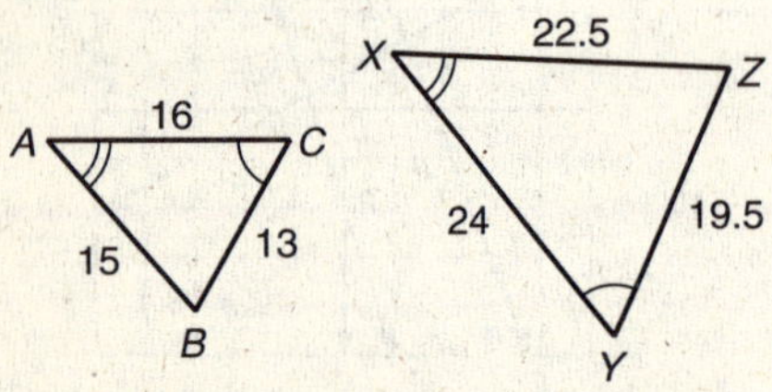

2.

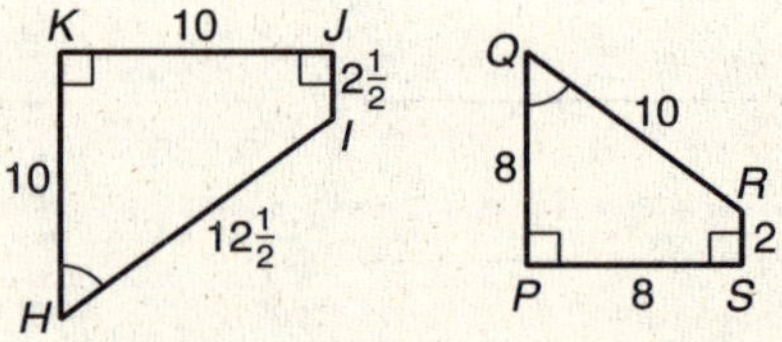

____

____

____

Determine whether the polygons are similar. If so, write the similarity ratio and a similarity statement. If not, explain why not.

3. parallelograms *EFGH* and *TUVW*

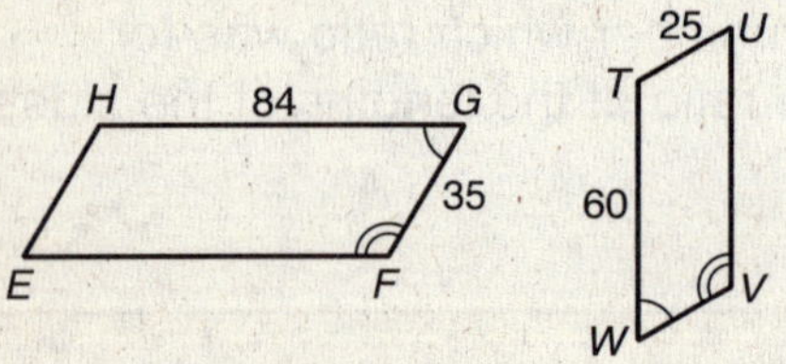

4. $\triangle CDE$ and $\triangle LMN$

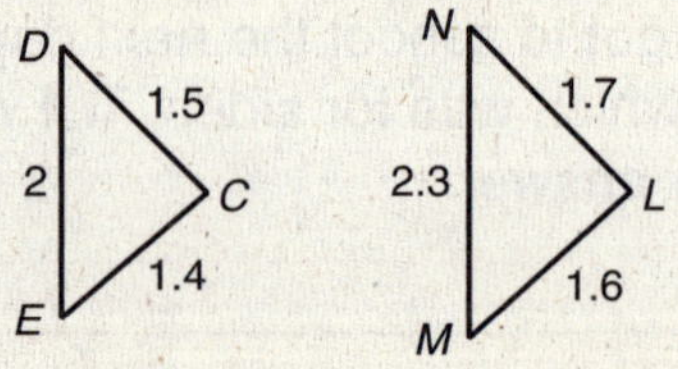

____

____

Tell whether the polygons must be similar based on the information given in the figures.

5.

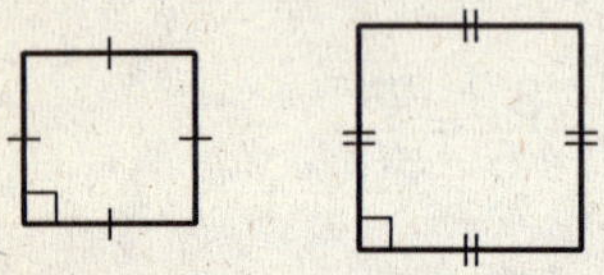

6.

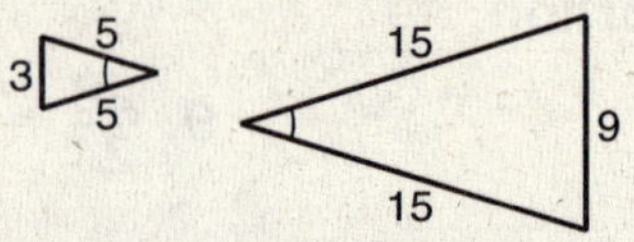

____

7.

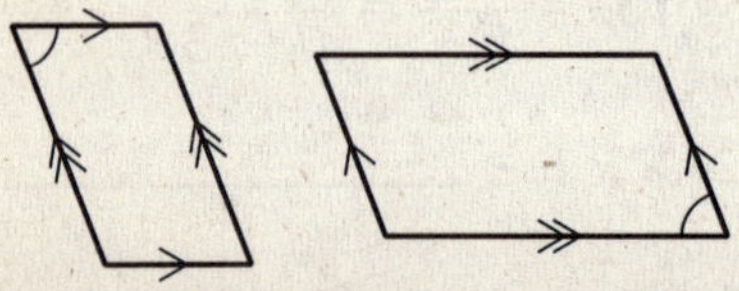

8.

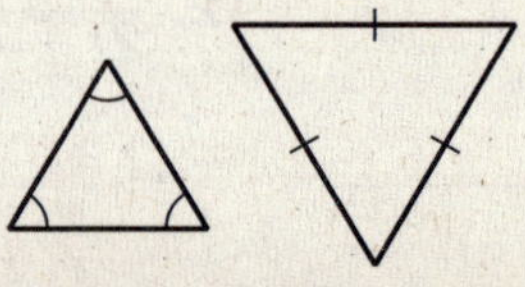

____

Name ______________________ Date __________ Class __________

LESSON 7-3

Practice B

Triangle Similarity: AA, SSS, SAS

For Exercises 1 and 2, explain why the triangles are similar and write a similarity statement.

1.

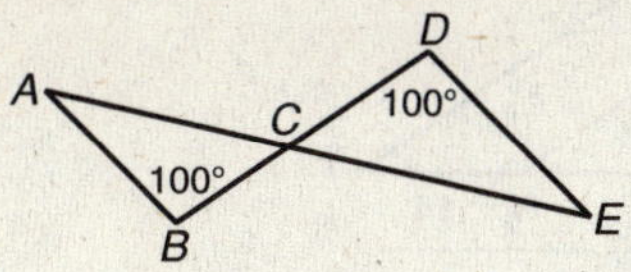

2.

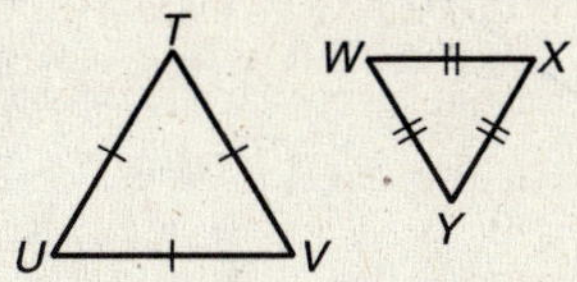

For Exercises 3 and 4, verify that the triangles are similar. Explain why.

3. $\triangle JLK$ and $\triangle JMN$

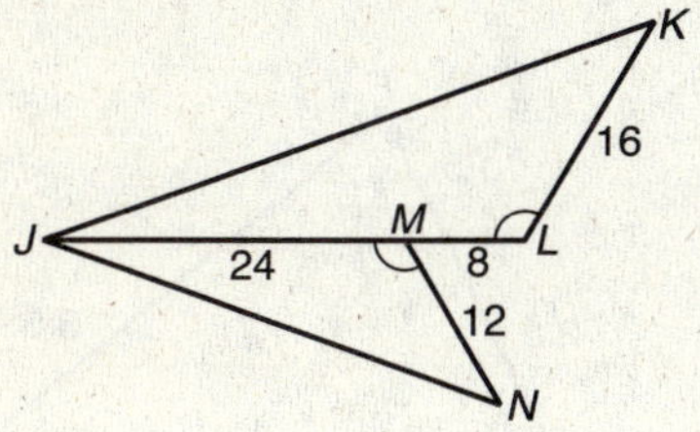

4. $\triangle PQR$ and $\triangle UTS$

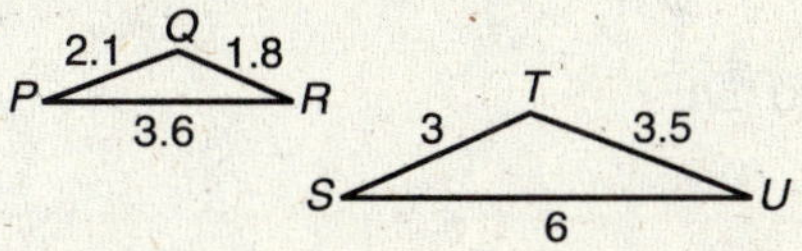

For Exercise 5, explain why the triangles are similar and find the stated length.

5. *DE*

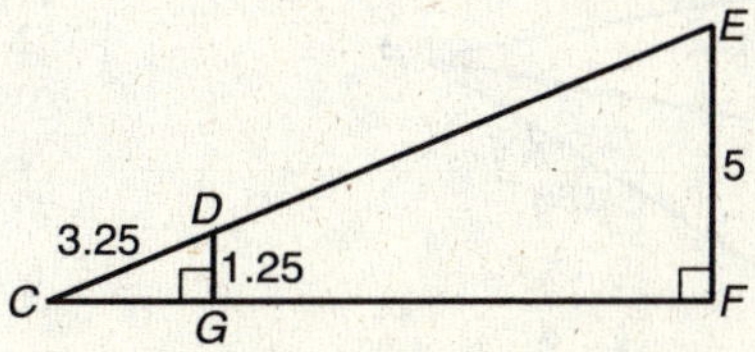

Name ______________________ Date ____________ Class ____________

LESSON 7-4

Practice B

Applying Properties of Similar Triangles

Find each length.

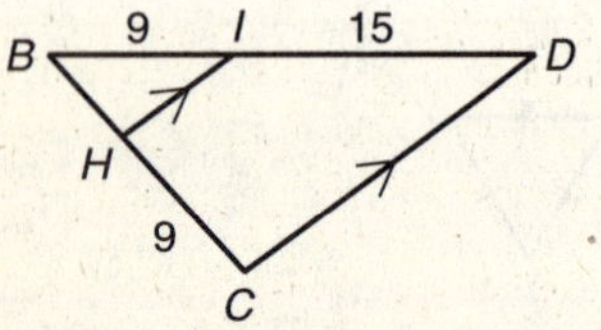

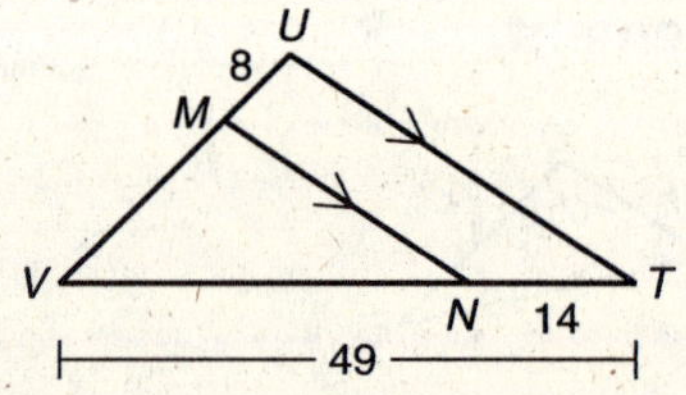

1. *BH* ____________________

2. *MV* ____________________

Verify that the given segments are parallel.

3. $\overline{PQ}$ and $\overline{NM}$

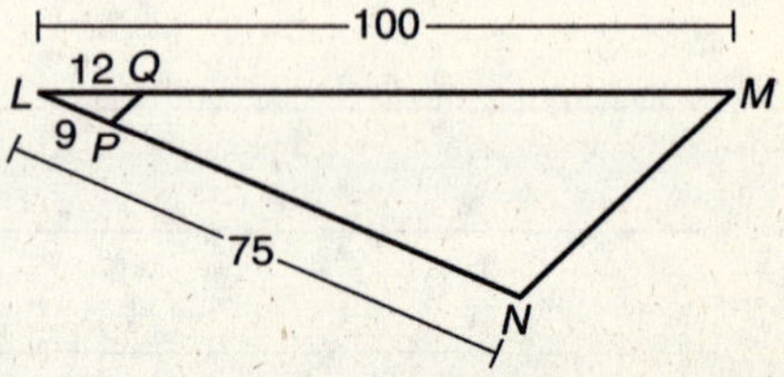

____

____

____

4. $\overline{WX}$ and $\overline{DE}$

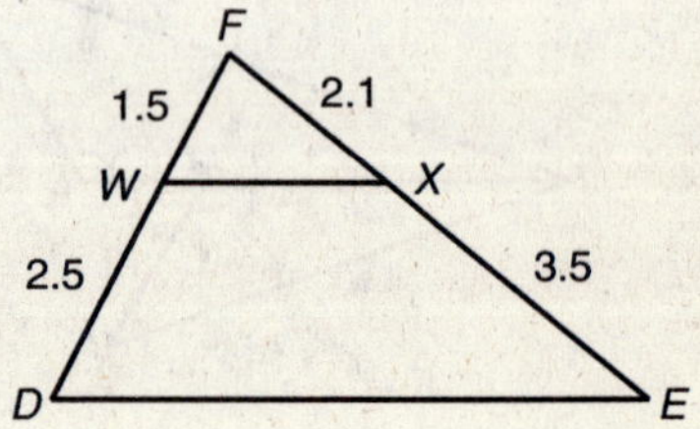

____

____

____

Find each length.

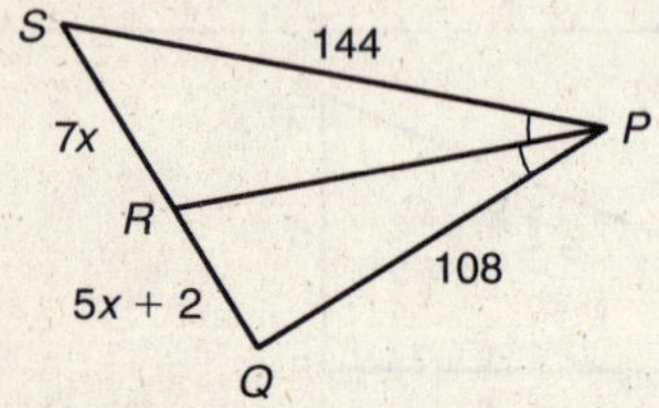

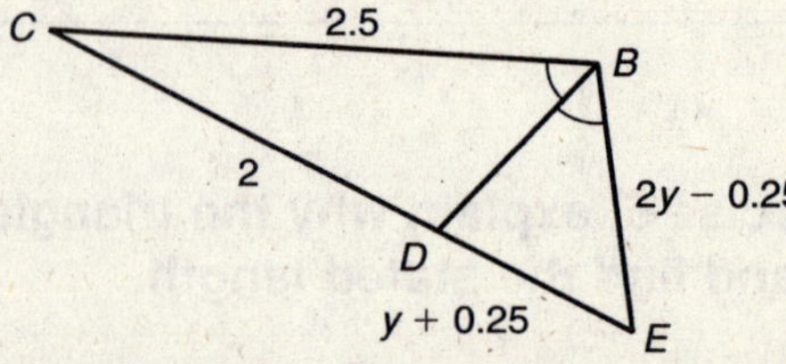

5. *SR* and *RQ* ____________________

6. *BE* and *DE* ____________________

7. In $\triangle ABC$, $\overline{BD}$ bisects $\angle ABC$ and $\overline{AD} \cong \overline{CD}$. Tell what kind of $\triangle ABC$ must be. ____________________

Name ______________________ Date ____________ Class ____________

LESSON 7-5

Practice B

Using Proportional Relationships

Refer to the figure for Exercises 1–3. A city is planning an outdoor concert for an Independence Day celebration. To hold speakers and lights, a crew of technicians sets up a scaffold with two platforms by the stage. The first platform is 8 feet 2 inches off the ground. The second platform is 7 feet 6 inches above the first platform. The shadow of the first platform stretches 6 feet 3 inches across the ground.

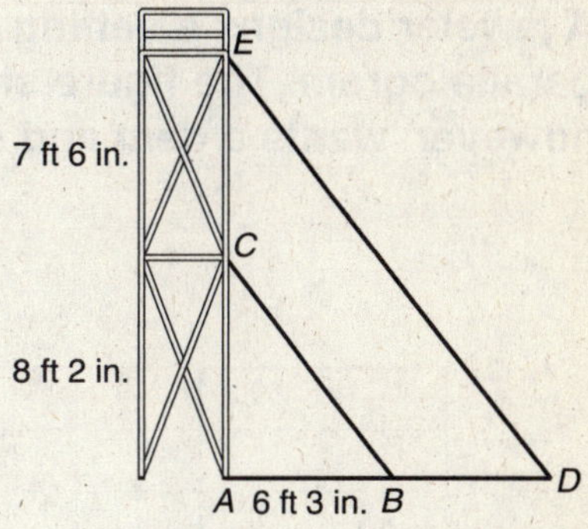

1. Explain why $\triangle ABC$ is similar to $\triangle ADE$. (*Hint:* The sun's rays are parallel.)

____

____

____

2. Find the length of the shadow of the second platform in feet and inches to the nearest inch. ____________

3. A 5-foot-8-inch-tall technician is standing on top of the second platform. Find the length of the shadow the scaffold and the technician cast in feet and inches to the nearest inch. ____________

Refer to the figure for Exercises 4–6. Ramona wants to renovate the kitchen in her house. The figure shows a blueprint of the new kitchen drawn to a scale of 1 cm : 2 ft. Use a centimeter ruler and the figure to find each actual measure in feet.

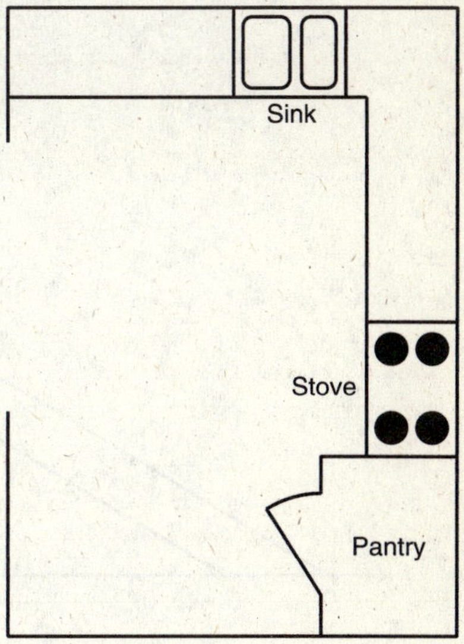

4. width of the kitchen ____________

5. length of the kitchen ____________

6. width of the sink ____________

7. area of the pantry ____________

Given that *DEFG* ~ *WXYZ*, find each of the following.

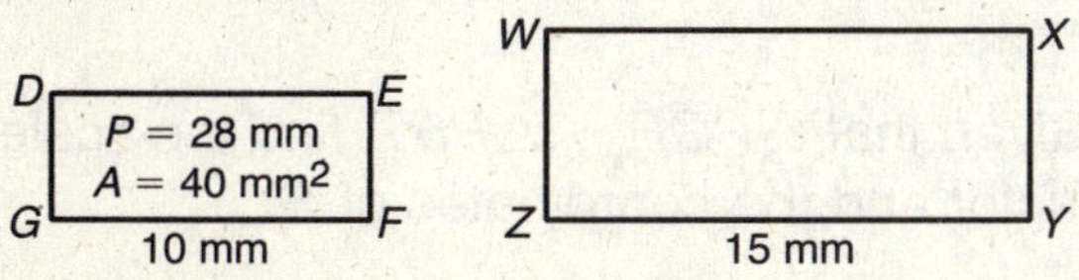

8. perimeter of *WXYZ* ____________

9. area of *WXYZ* ____________

Name ________________________________ Date ____________ Class ____________

LESSON **7-6**

Practice B

Dilations and Similarity in the Coordinate Plane

A jeweler designs a setting that can hold a gem in the shape of a parallelogram. The figure shows the outline of the gem. The client, however, wants a gem and setting that is slightly larger.

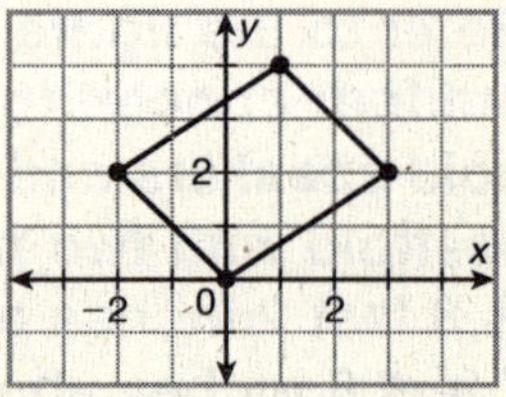

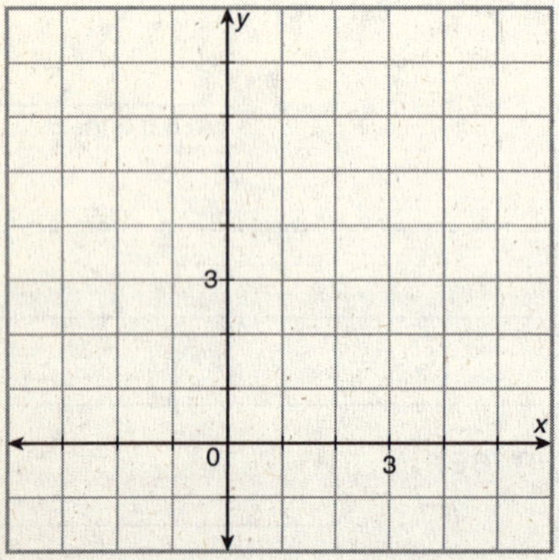

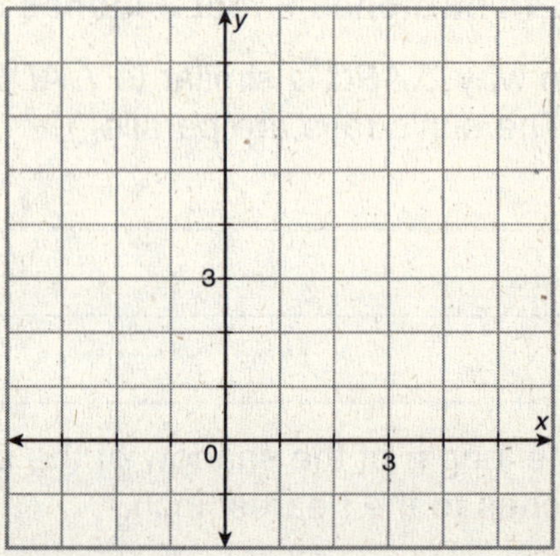

1. Draw the gem after a dilation with a scale factor of $\frac{3}{2}$.

2. The client is so pleased with her ring that she decides to have matching but smaller earrings made using the same pattern. Draw the gem after a dilation from the original pattern with a scale factor of $\frac{1}{2}$.

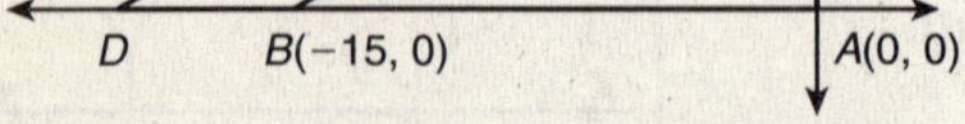

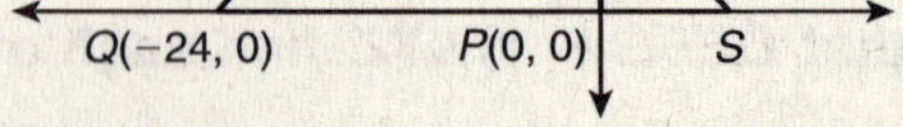

3. Given that $\triangle ABC \sim \triangle ADE$, find the scale factor and the coordinates of D.

____

4. Given that $\triangle PQR \sim \triangle PST$, find the scale factor and the coordinates of S.

____

Name ______________________ Date ____________ Class ____________

LESSON 8-1

Practice B
Similarity in Right Triangles

Write a similarity statement comparing the three triangles in each diagram.

1.

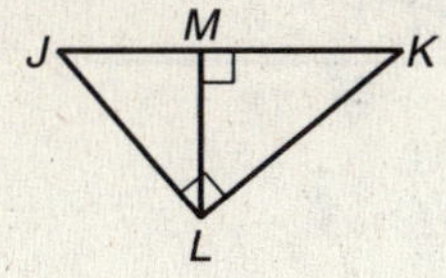

2.

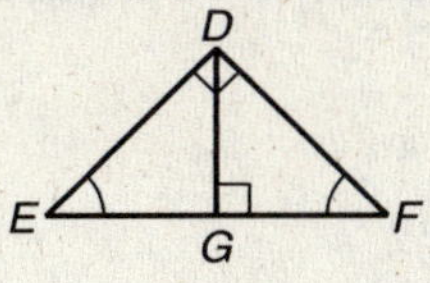

3.

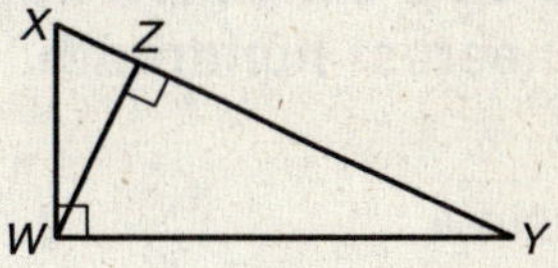

________________ ________________ ________________

________________ ________________ ________________

Find the geometric mean of each pair of numbers. If necessary, give the answer in simplest radical form.

4. $\frac{1}{4}$ and 4 ________

5. 3 and 75 ________

6. 4 and 18 ________

7. $\frac{1}{2}$ and 9 ________

8. 10 and 14 ________

9. 4 and 12.25 ________

Find *x*, *y*, and *z*.

10.

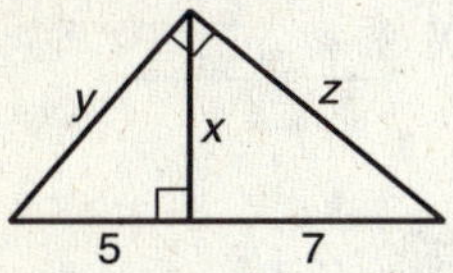

11.

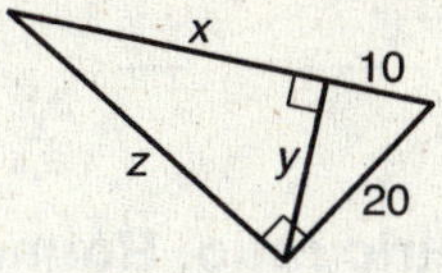

12.

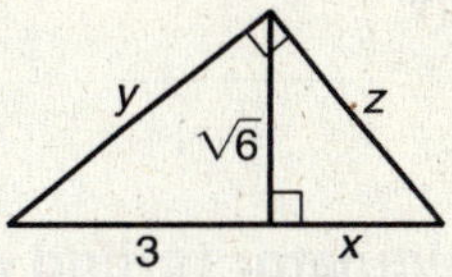

________________ ________________ ________________

13.

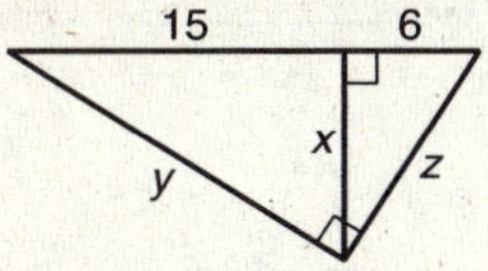

14.

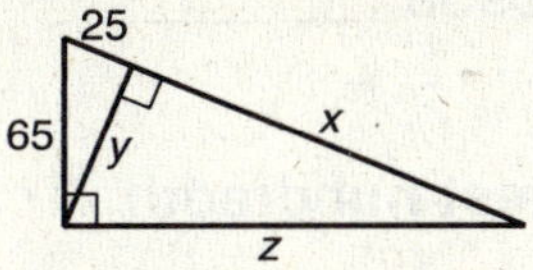

15.

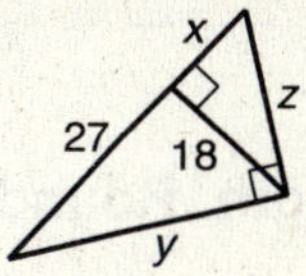

________________ ________________ ________________

16. The Coast Guard has sent a rescue helicopter to retrieve passengers off a disabled ship. The ship has called in its position as 1.7 miles from shore. When the helicopter passes over a buoy that is known to be 1.3 miles from shore, the angle formed by the shore, the helicopter, and the disabled ship is 90°. Determine what the altimeter would read to the nearest foot when the helicopter is directly above the buoy.

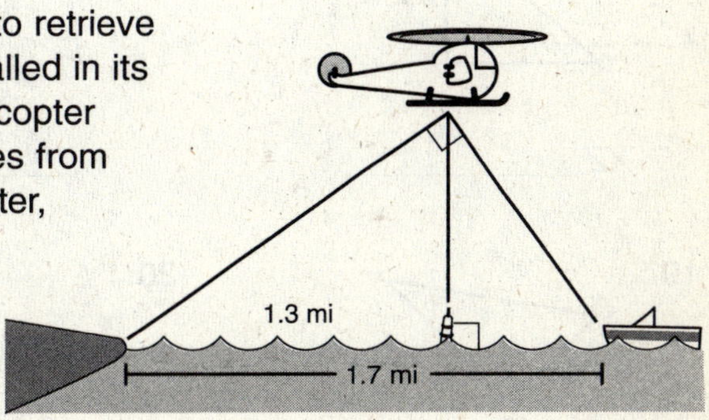

____

Use the diagram to complete each equation.

17. $\frac{e}{b} = \frac{\square}{e}$

18. $\frac{d}{b + c} = \frac{\square}{a}$

19. $\frac{d}{\square} = \frac{a}{e}$

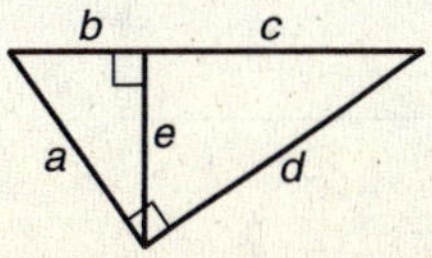

Name ______________________ Date __________ Class __________

LESSON 8-2

Practice B
Trigonometric Ratios

Use the figure for Exercises 1–6. Write each trigonometric ratio as a simplified fraction and as a decimal rounded to the nearest hundredth.

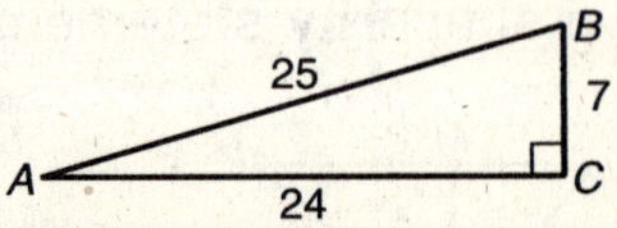

1. sin *A* ______________
2. cos *B* ______________
3. tan *B* ______________
4. sin *B* ______________
5. cos *A* ______________
6. tan *A* ______________

Use special right triangles to write each trigonometric ratio as a simplified fraction.

7. sin 30° __________
8. cos 30° __________
9. tan 45° __________
10. tan 30° __________
11. cos 45° __________
12. tan 60° __________

Use a calculator to find each trigonometric ratio. Round to the nearest hundredth.

13. sin 64° __________
14. cos 58° __________
15. tan 15° __________

Find each length. Round to the nearest hundredth.

16.

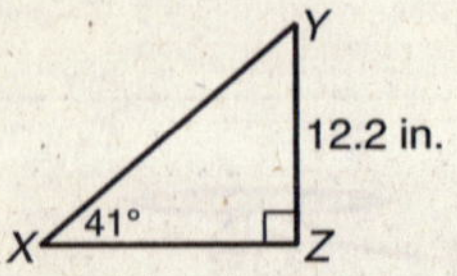

XZ __________

17.

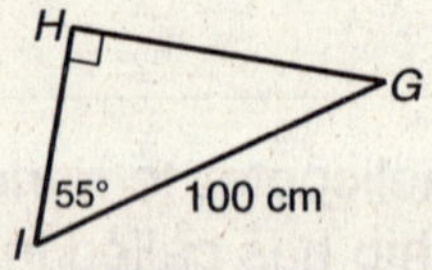

HI __________

18.

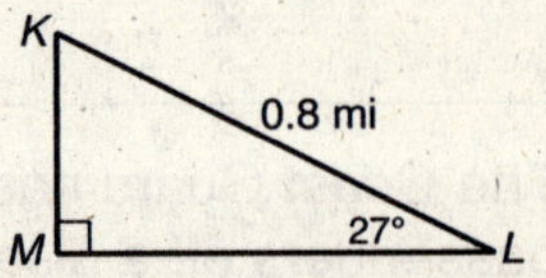

KM __________

19.

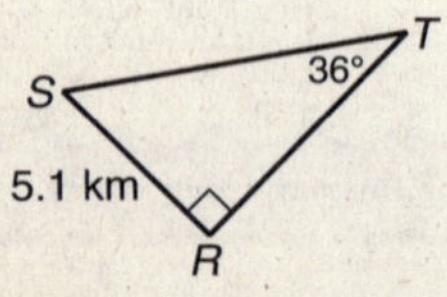

ST __________

20.

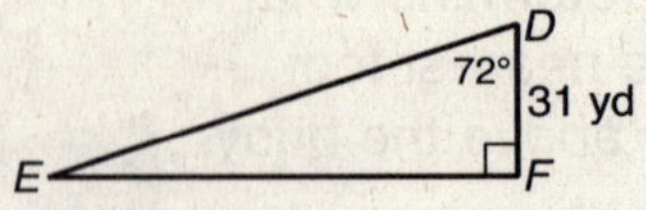

EF __________

21.

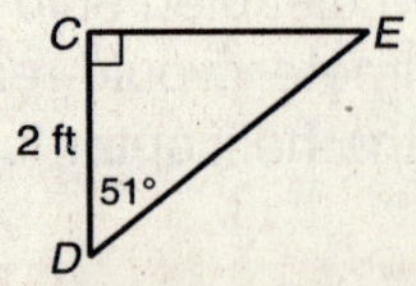

DE __________

Name ______________________ Date ____________ Class ____________

LESSON 8-3

Practice B
Solving Right Triangles

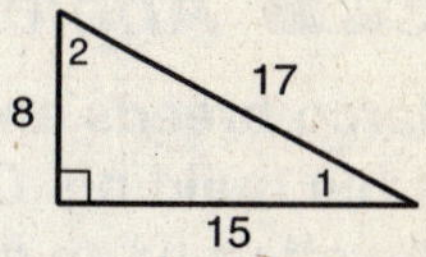

Use the given trigonometric ratio to determine which angle of the triangle is $\angle A$.

1. $\sin A = \frac{8}{17}$ ________
2. $\cos A = \frac{15}{17}$ ________
3. $\tan A = \frac{15}{8}$ ________
4. $\sin A = \frac{15}{17}$ ________
5. $\cos A = \frac{8}{17}$ ________
6. $\tan A = \frac{8}{15}$ ________

Use a calculator to find each angle measure to the nearest degree.

7. $\sin^{-1}(0.82)$ ________
8. $\cos^{-1}\left(\frac{11}{12}\right)$ ________
9. $\tan^{-1}(5.03)$ ________
10. $\sin^{-1}\left(\frac{3}{8}\right)$ ________
11. $\cos^{-1}(0.23)$ ________
12. $\tan^{-1}\left(\frac{1}{9}\right)$ ________

Find the unknown measures. Round lengths to the nearest hundredth and angle measures to the nearest degree.

13.

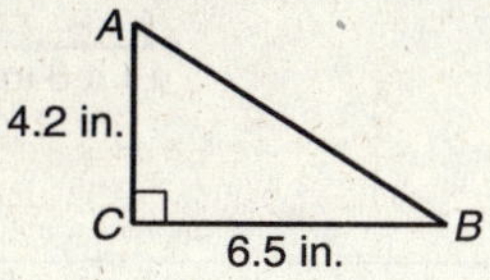

____

____

14.

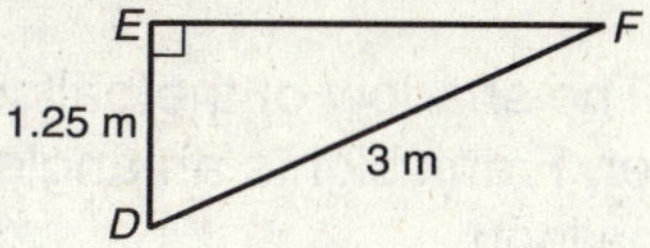

____

____

15.

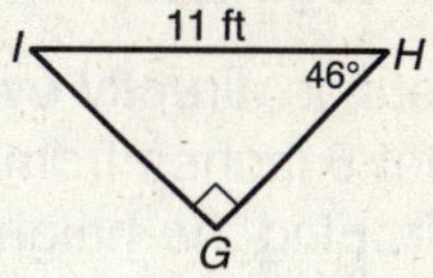

____

____

16.

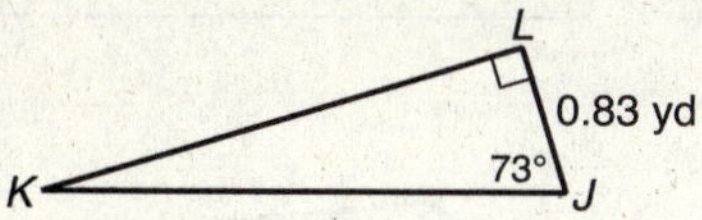

____

____

17.

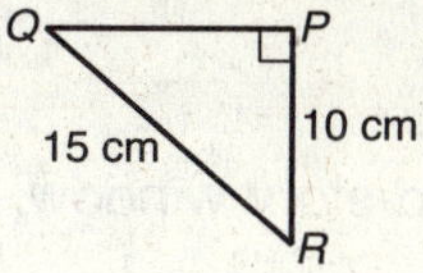

____

____

18.

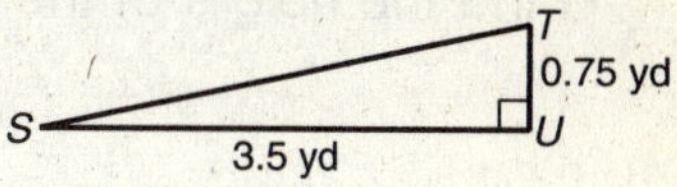

____

____

For each triangle, find all three side lengths to the nearest hundredth and all three angle measures to the nearest degree.

19. $B(-2, -4)$, $C(3, 3)$, $D(-2, 3)$

____

20. $L(-1, -6)$, $M(1, -6)$, $N(-1, 1)$

____

21. $X(-4, 5)$, $Y(-3, 5)$, $Z(-3, 4)$

____

Name ______________________________ Date ____________ Class ____________

LESSON 8-4

Practice B

Angles of Elevation and Depression

Marco breeds and trains homing pigeons on the roof of his building. Classify each angle as an angle of elevation or an angle of depression.

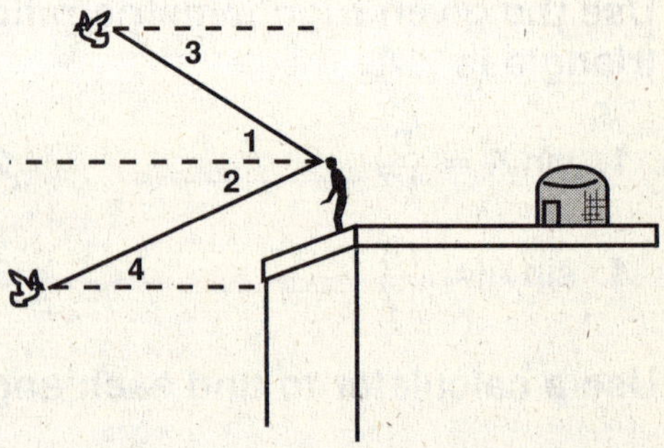

1. ∠1 ____________________

2. ∠2 ____________________

3. ∠3 ____________________

4. ∠4 ____________________

To attract customers to his car dealership, Frank tethers a large red balloon to the ground. In Exercises 5–7, give answers in feet and inches to the nearest inch. (*Note:* Assume the cord that attaches to the balloon makes a straight segment.)

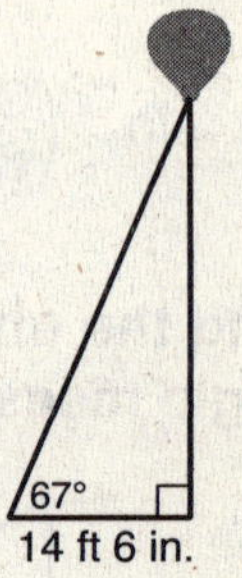

5. The sun is directly overhead. The shadow of the balloon falls 14 feet 6 inches from the tether. Frank sights an angle of elevation of 67°. Find the height of the balloon. ____________________

6. Find the length of the cord that tethers the balloon. ____________________

7. The wind picks up and the angle of elevation changes to 59°. Find the height of the balloon. ____________________

Lindsey shouts down to Pete from her third-story window.

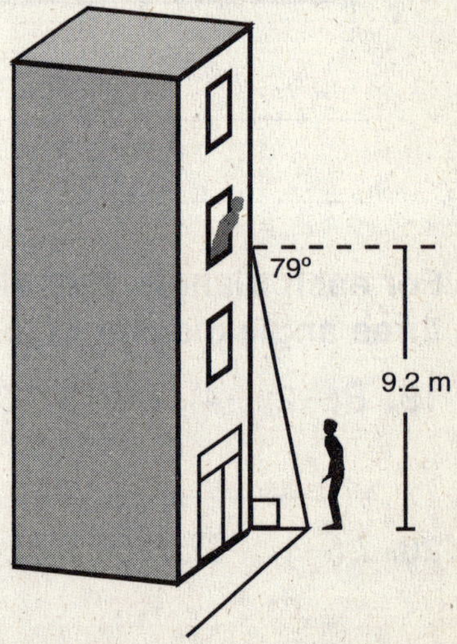

8. Lindsey is 9.2 meters up, and the angle of depression from Lindsey to Pete is 79°. Find the distance from Pete to the base of the building to the nearest tenth of a meter.

____

9. To see Lindsey better, Pete walks out into the street so he is 4.3 meters from the base of the building. Find the angle of depression from Lindsey to Pete to the nearest degree.

____

10. Mr. Shea lives in Lindsey's building. While Pete is still out in the street, Mr. Shea leans out his window to tell Lindsey and Pete to stop all the shouting. The angle of elevation from Pete to Mr. Shea is 72°. Tell whether Mr. Shea lives above or below Lindsey.

____

Name ________________________ Date ____________ Class ____________

LESSON 8-5

Practice B

Law of Sines and Law of Cosines

Use a calculator to find each trigonometric ratio. Round to the nearest hundredth.

1. sin 111° ________ **2.** cos 150° ________ **3.** tan 163° ________

4. sin 92° ________ **5.** cos 129° ________ **6.** tan 99° ________

7. sin 170° ________ **8.** cos 96° ________ **9.** tan 117° ________

Use the Law of Sines to find each measure. Round lengths to the nearest tenth and angle measures to the nearest degree.

10.

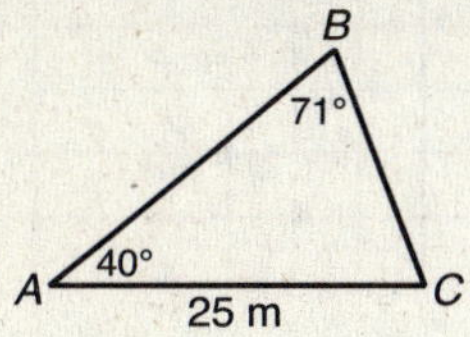

BC ________

11.

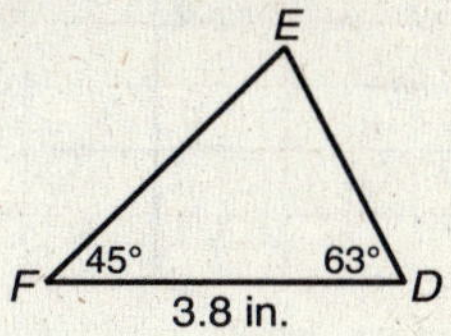

DE ________

12.

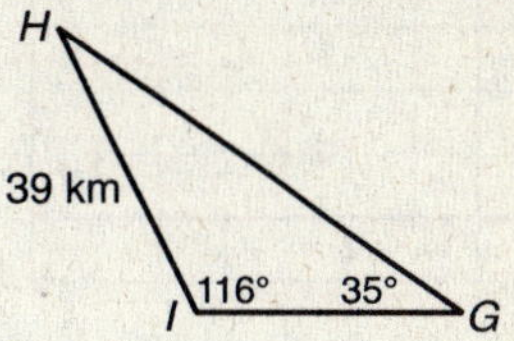

GH ________

13.

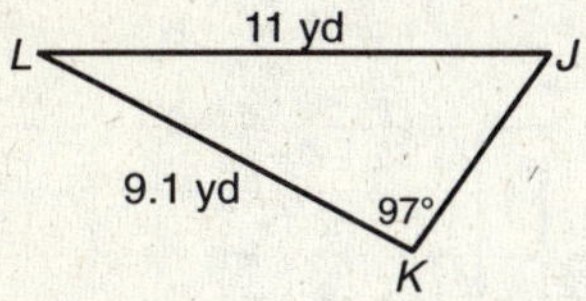

m∠*J* ________

14.

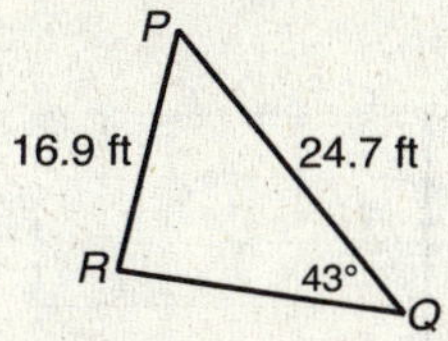

m∠*R* ________

15.

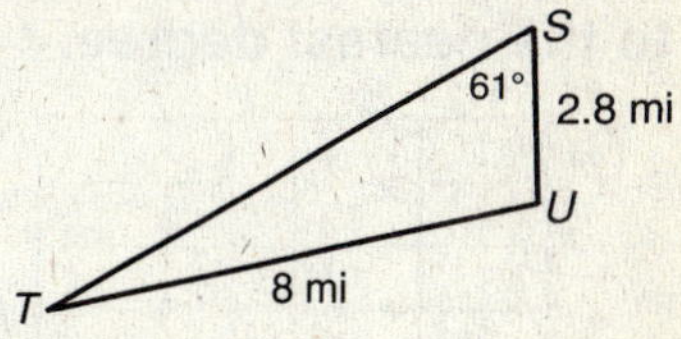

m∠*T* ________

Use the Law of Cosines to find each measure. Round lengths to the nearest tenth and angle measures to the nearest degree.

16.

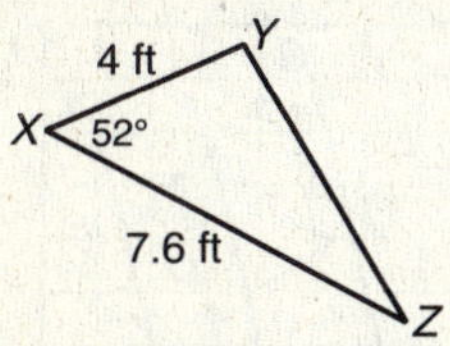

YZ ________

17.

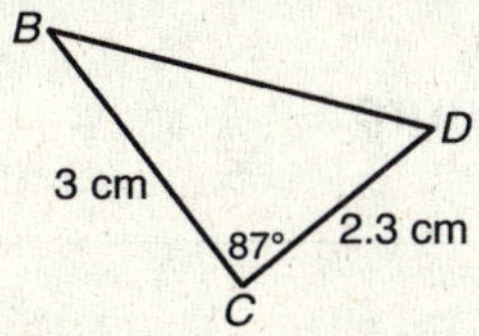

BD ________

18.

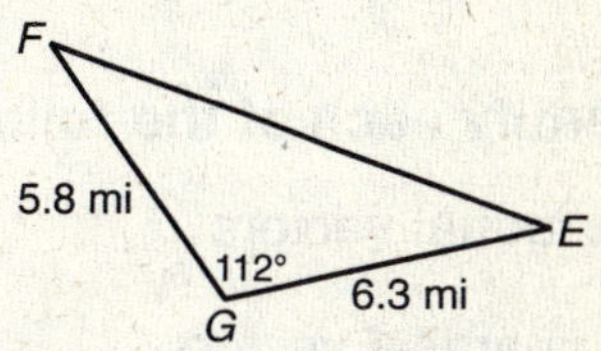

EF ________

19.

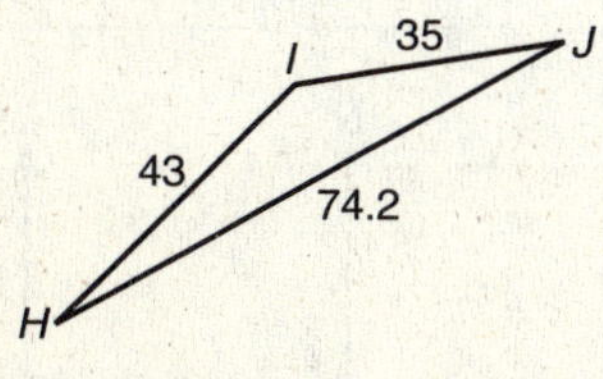

m∠*I* ________

20.

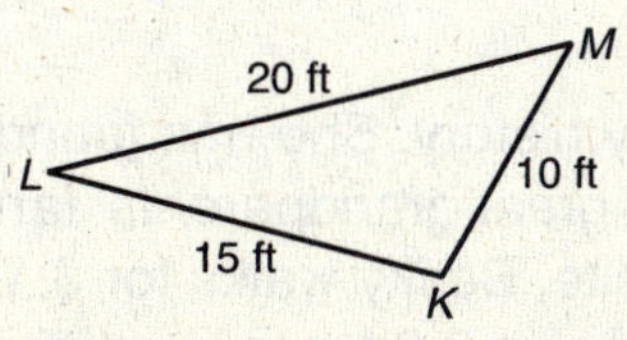

m∠*M* ________

21.

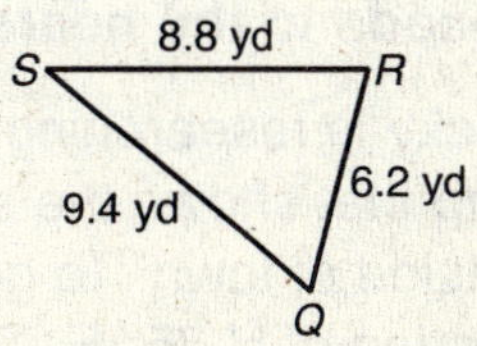

m∠*S* ________

Name ______________________ Date ____________ Class ____________

LESSON **8-6**

Practice B
Vectors

Write each vector in component form.

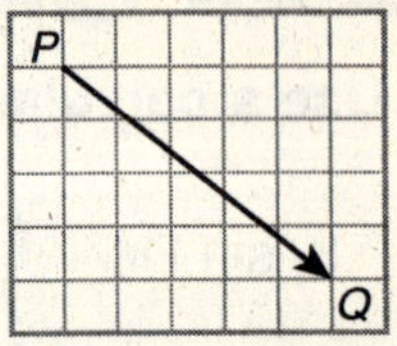

1. $\overrightarrow{PQ}$ ____________________

2. $\overrightarrow{EF}$ with $E(-1, 2)$ and $F(-10, -3)$ ____________________

3. the vector with initial point $V(7, 3)$ and terminal point $W(0, -1)$ ____________________

Draw each vector on a coordinate plane. Find its magnitude to the nearest tenth.

4. 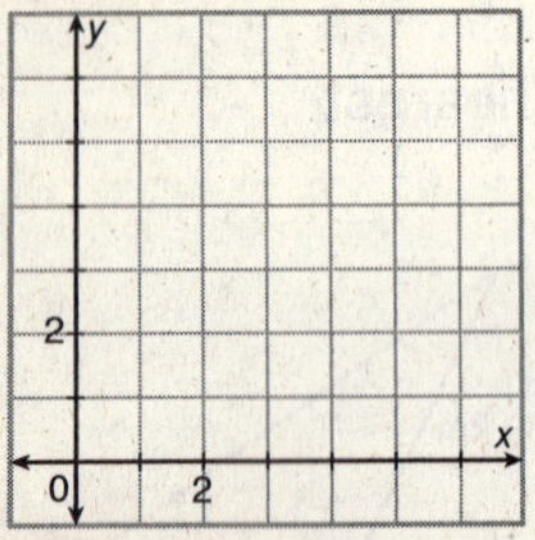

$\langle 5, 2\rangle$ __________

5. 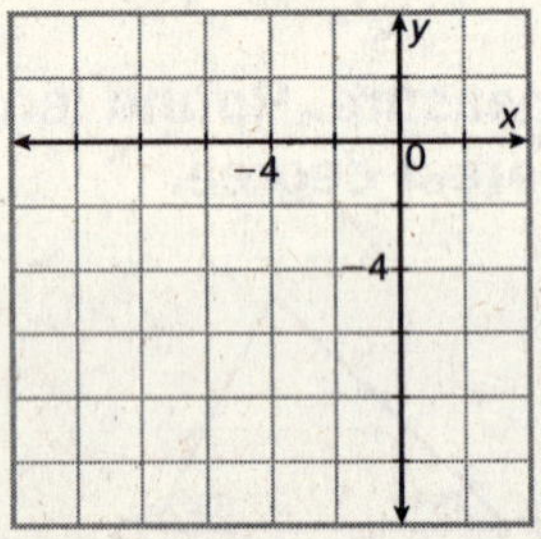

$\langle -4, -7\rangle$ __________

6. 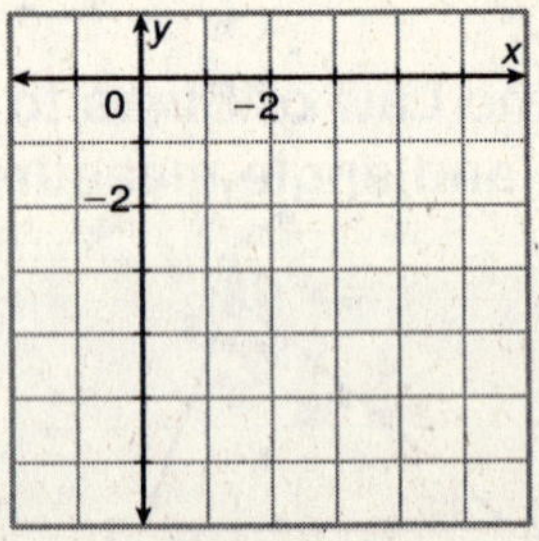

$\langle 3, -6\rangle$ __________

Draw each vector on a coordinate plane. Find the direction of the vector to the nearest degree.

7. 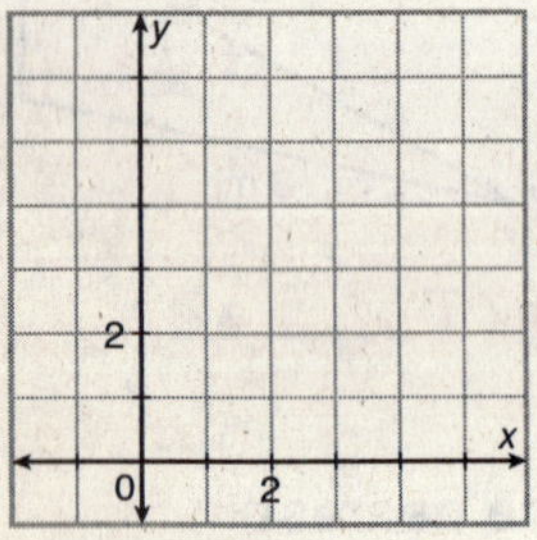

$\langle 4, 6\rangle$ __________

8. 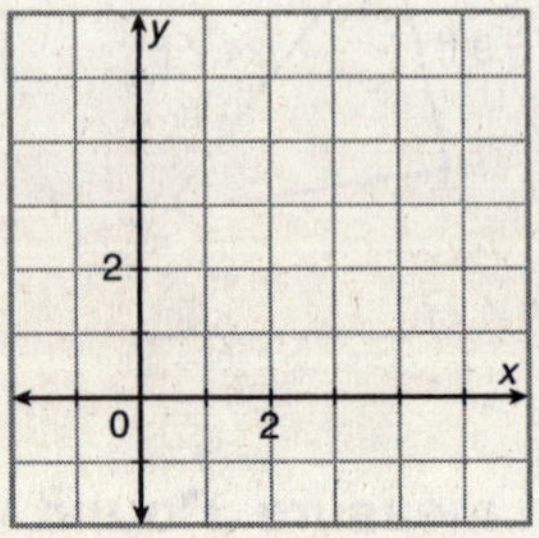

$\langle 3, 2\rangle$ __________

9. 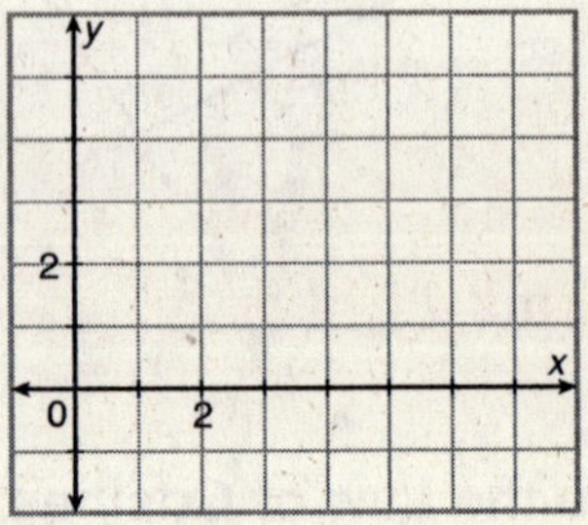

$\langle 7, 2\rangle$ __________

Identify each of the following in the figure.

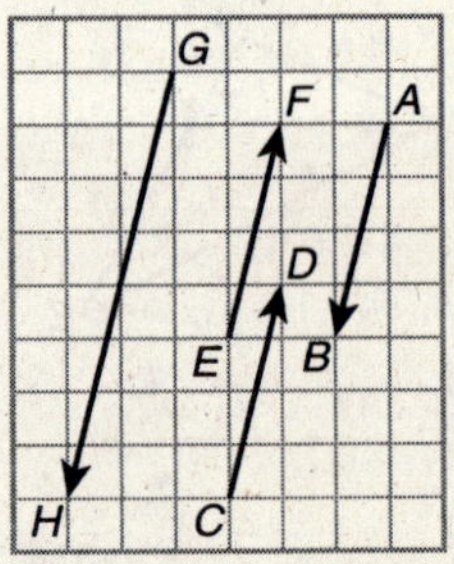

10. equal vectors ______________________________

11. parallel vectors ______________________________

In Exercise 12, round directions to the nearest degree and speeds to the nearest tenth.

12. Becky is researching her family history. She has found an old map that shows the site of her great grandparents' farmhouse outside of town. To get to the site, Becky walks for 3.1 km at a bearing of N 75° E. Then she walks 2.2 km due north. Find the distance and direction Becky could have walked to get straight to the site.

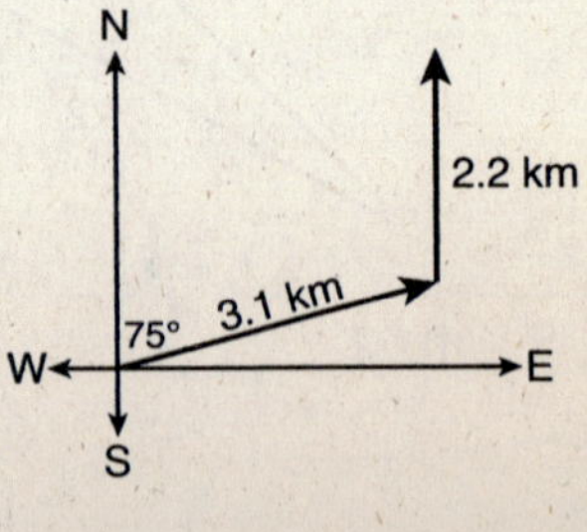

____

Name ______________________________ Date ____________ Class ____________

LESSON 9-1

Practice B

Developing Formulas for Triangles and Quadrilaterals

Find each measurement.

1. 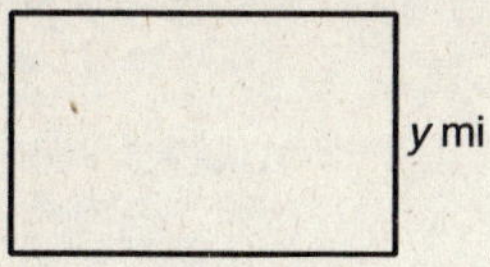

the perimeter of the rectangle in which $A = 2xy\text{ mi}^2$

____

2. 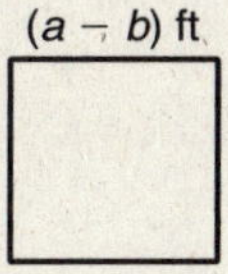

the area of the square

____

3. the height of a parallelogram in which $A = 96\text{ cm}^2$ and $b = 8x$ cm ________________________

4. 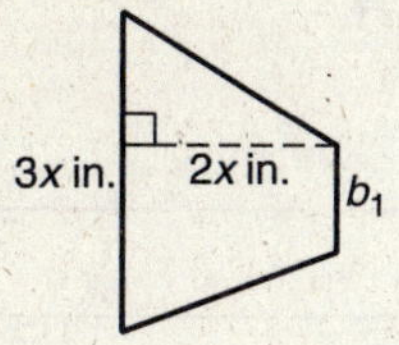

b_1 of the trapezoid in which $A = 4x^2\text{ in}^2$

____

5. 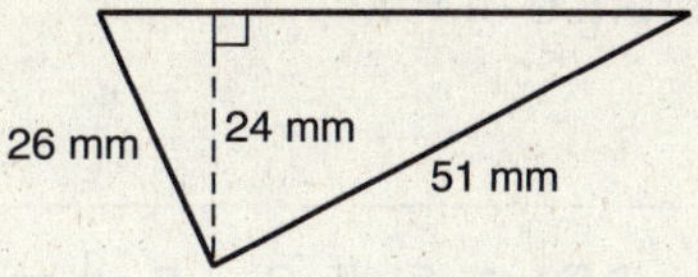

the area of the triangle

____

6. the area of a trapezoid in which $b_1 = 3a$ km, $b_2 = 6a$ km, and $h = (10 + 4c)$ km

____

7. 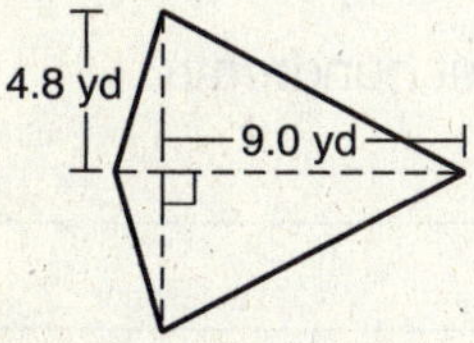

the perimeter of the kite in which $A = 49.92\text{ yd}^2$

____

8. 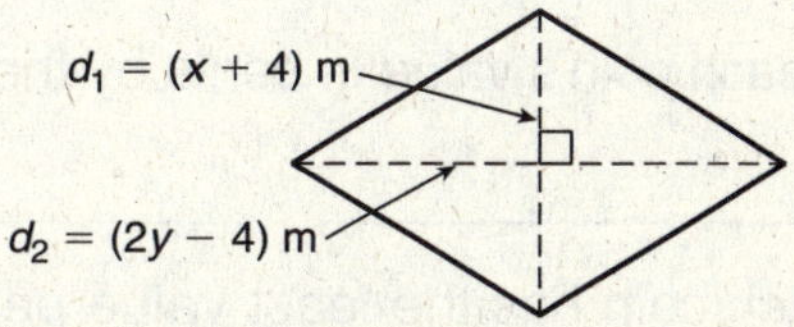

the area of the rhombus

____

9. d_2 of the kite in which $d_1 = (a - 4)$ ft and $A = (2a^2 - 8a)\text{ ft}^2$

____

Name ______________________ Date ____________ Class ____________

LESSON **9-2**

Practice B

Developing Formulas for Circles and Regular Polygons

Find each measurement. Give your answers in terms of π.

1. 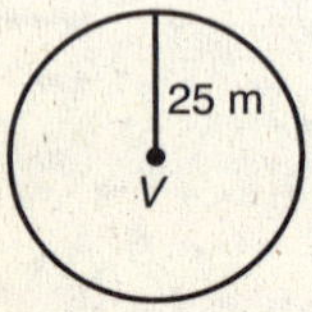

the area of $\odot V$

____

2. 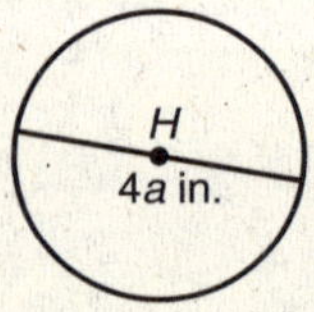

the area of $\odot H$

____

3. 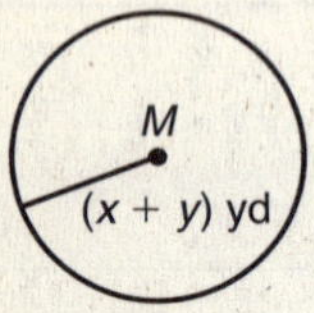

the circumference of $\odot M$

____

4. 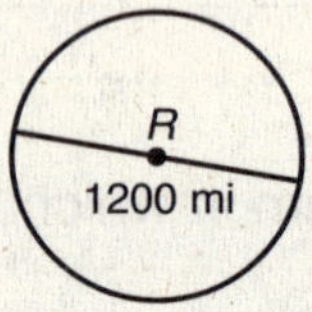

the circumference of $\odot R$

____

5. the radius of $\odot D$ in which $C = 2\pi^2$ cm ________________________

6. the diameter of $\odot K$ in which $A = (x^2 + 2x + 1)\pi$ km^2 ________________________

Stella wants to cover a tabletop with nickels, dimes, or quarters. She decides to find which coin would cost the least to use.

7. Stella measures the diameters of a nickel, a dime, and a quarter. They are 21.2 mm, 17.8 mm, and 24.5 mm. Find the areas of the nickel, the dime, and the quarter. Round to the nearest tenth.

____

8. Divide each coin's value in cents by the coin's area. Round to the nearest hundredth.

____

9. Tell which coin has the least value per unit of area. ________________________

10. Tell about how many nickels would cover a square tabletop that measures 1 square meter. Then find the cost of the coins.

____

Find the area of each regular polygon. Round to the nearest tenth.

11. 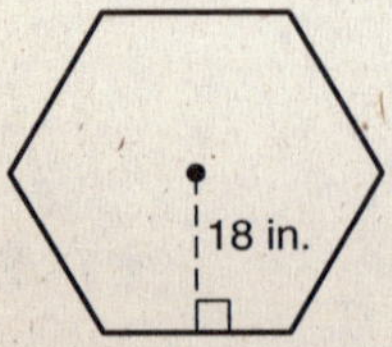

____

12. 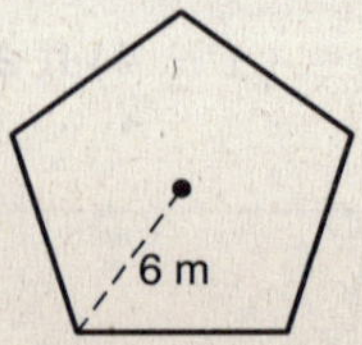

____

Name ______________________ Date ____________ Class ____________

LESSON **9-3**

Practice B

Composite Figures

Find the shaded area. Round to the nearest tenth if necessary.

1.

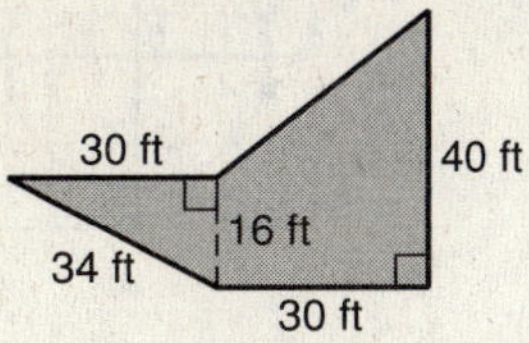

____

2.

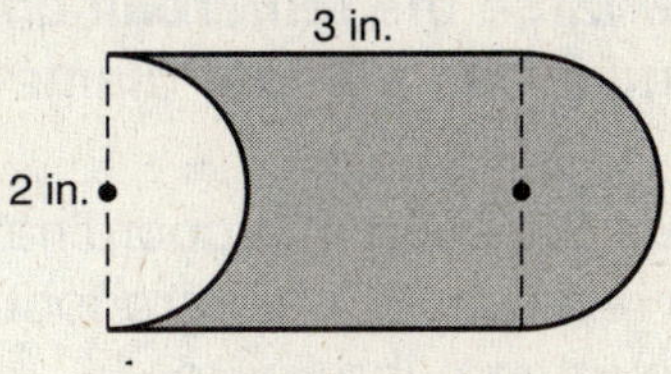

____

3.

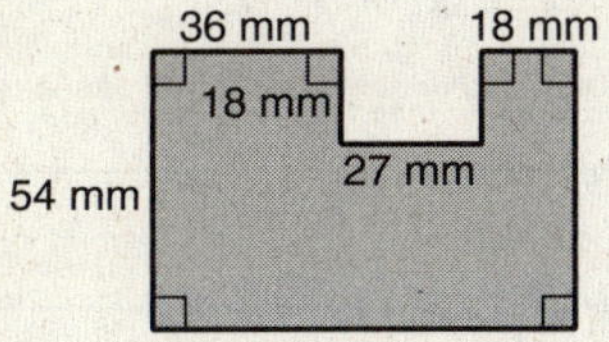

____

4.

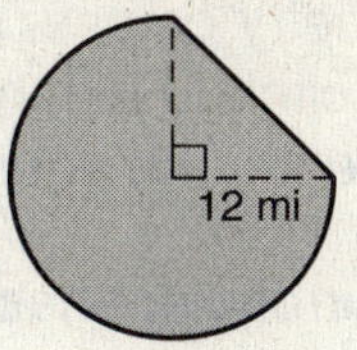

____

5.

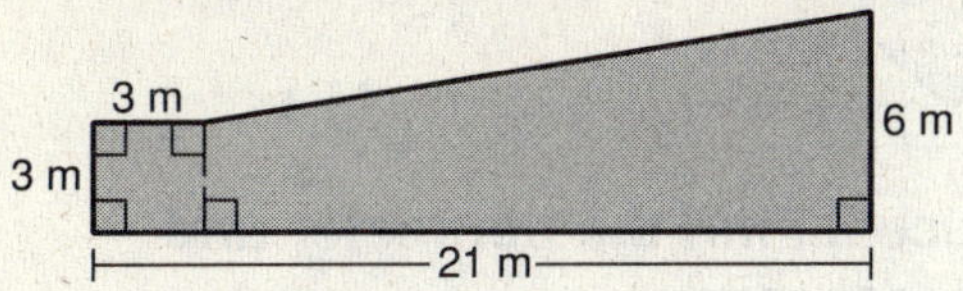

____

6.

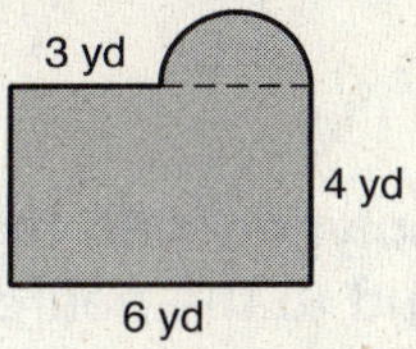

____

7.

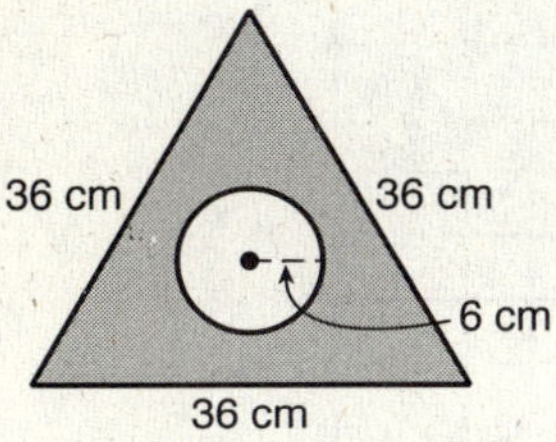

____

8.

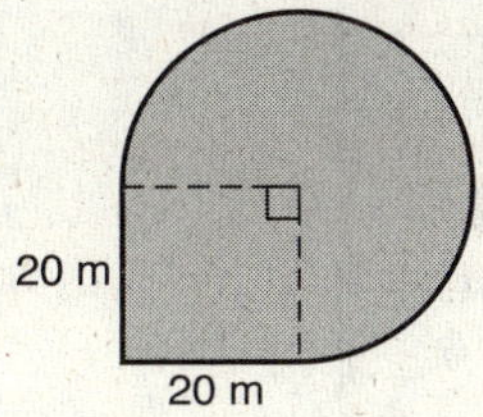

____

9. Osman broke the unusually shaped picture window in his parents' living room. The figure shows the dimensions of the window. Replacement glass costs $8 per square foot, and there will be a $35 installation fee. Find the cost to replace the window to the nearest cent.

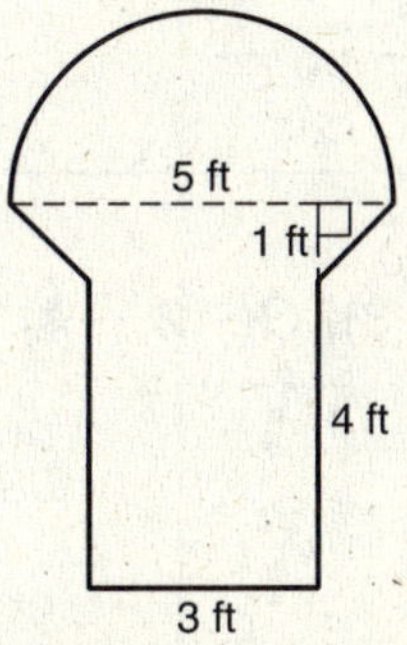

____

Estimate the area of each shaded irregular shape. The grid has squares with side lengths of 1 cm.

10.

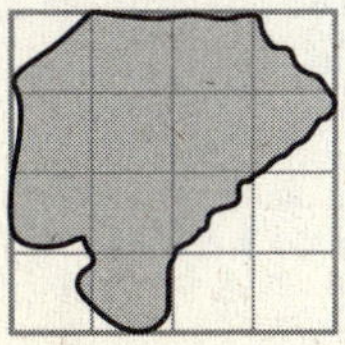

____

11.

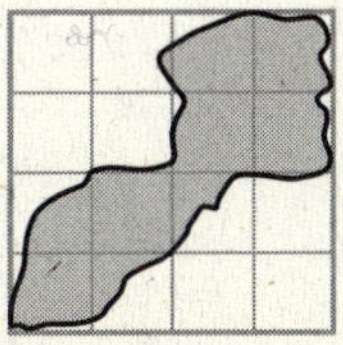

____

Name ______________________________ Date ____________ Class ____________

LESSON **9-4**

Practice B

Perimeter and Area in the Coordinate Plane

Lena and her older sister Margie love to play tetherball. They want to find how large the tetherball court is. They measure the court and find it has a 6-foot diameter.

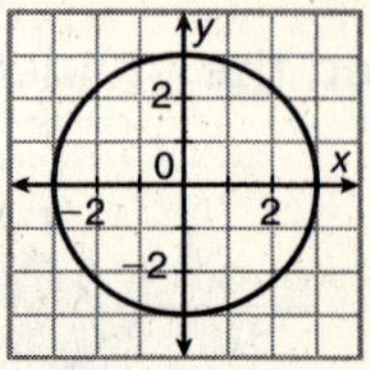

1. Lena sketches the court in a coordinate plane in which each square represents 1 square foot. Estimate the size of the court from the figure. ________________

2. Margie has taken a geometry course, so she knows the formula for the area of a circle. Find the actual area of the court to the nearest tenth of a square foot. ________________

3. Estimate the area of the irregular shape. ________________

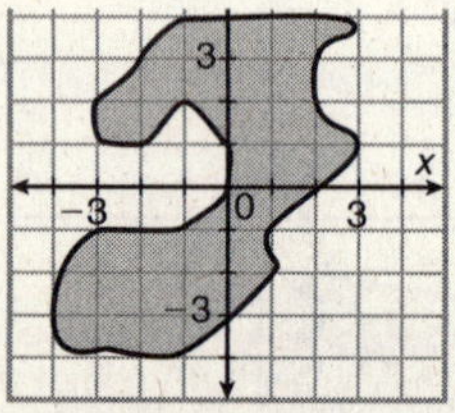

Draw and classify each polygon with the given vertices. Find the perimeter and area of the polygon. Round to the nearest tenth if necessary.

4. $A(-2, 3)$, $B(3, 1)$, $C(-2, -1)$, $D(-3, 1)$

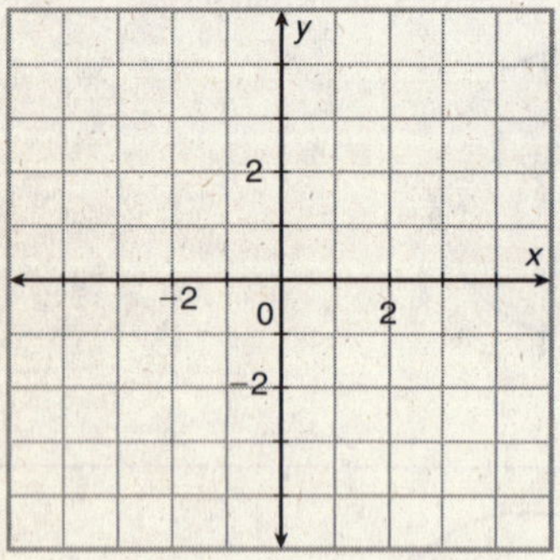

____

5. $P(-3, -4)$, $Q(3, -3)$, $R(3, -2)$, $S(-3, 2)$

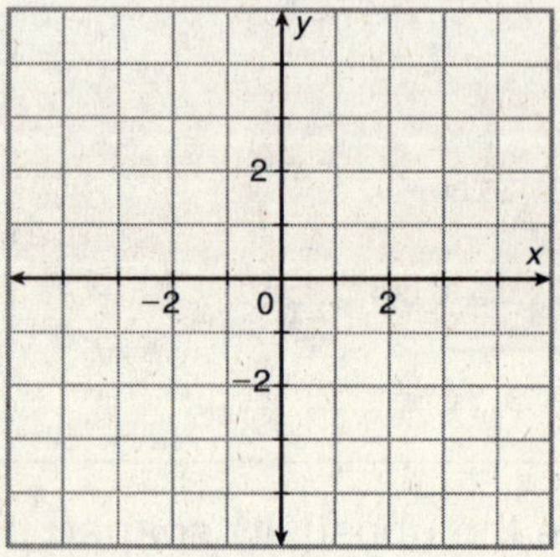

____

6. $E(-4, 1)$, $F(-2, 3)$, $G(-2, -4)$

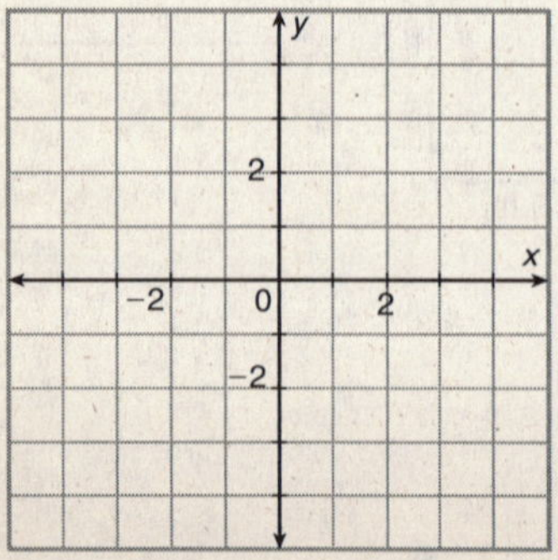

____

7. $T(1, -2)$, $U(4, 1)$, $V(2, 3)$, $W(-1, 0)$

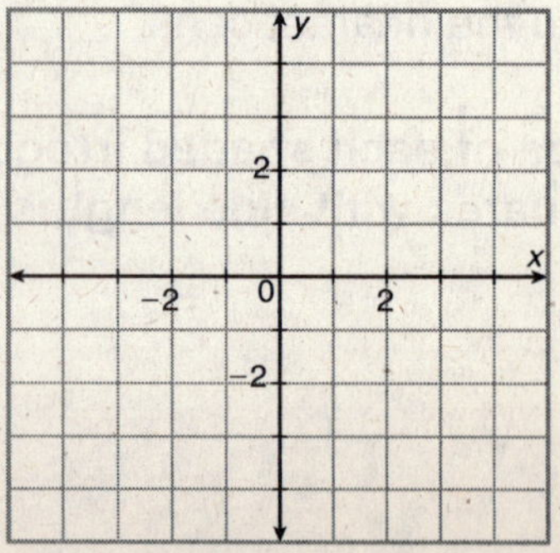

____

Name ______________________ Date ____________ Class ____________

LESSON **9-5**

Practice B

Effects of Changing Dimensions Proportionally

Describe the effect of each change on the area of the given figure.

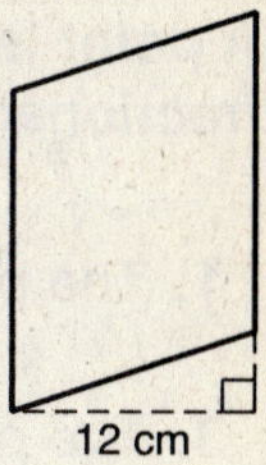

1. The base of the parallelogram is multiplied by $\frac{3}{4}$.

2. The length of a rectangle with length 12 yd and width 11 yd is divided by 6.

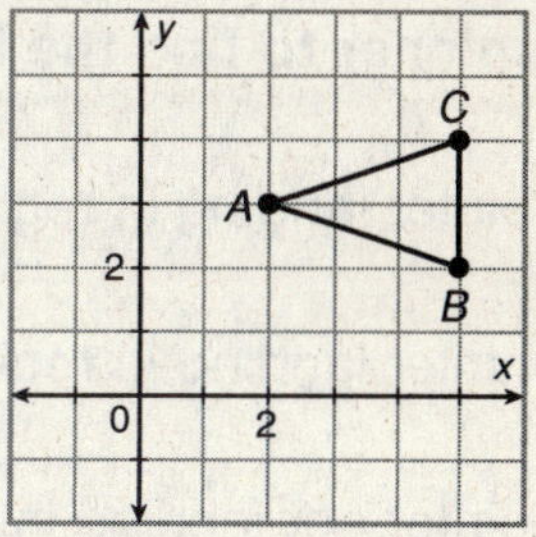

3. The base of a triangle with vertices $A(2, 3)$, $B(5, 2)$, and $C(5, 4)$ is doubled.

4. The height of a trapezoid with base lengths 4 mm and 7 mm and height 9 mm is multiplied by $\frac{1}{3}$.

In Exercises 5–8, describe the effect of each change on the perimeter or circumference and the area of the given figure.

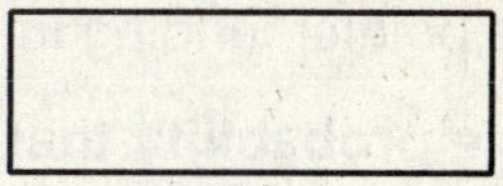

5. The length and width of the rectangle are multiplied by $\frac{4}{3}$.

6. The base and height of a triangle with base 1.5 m and height 6 m are both tripled.

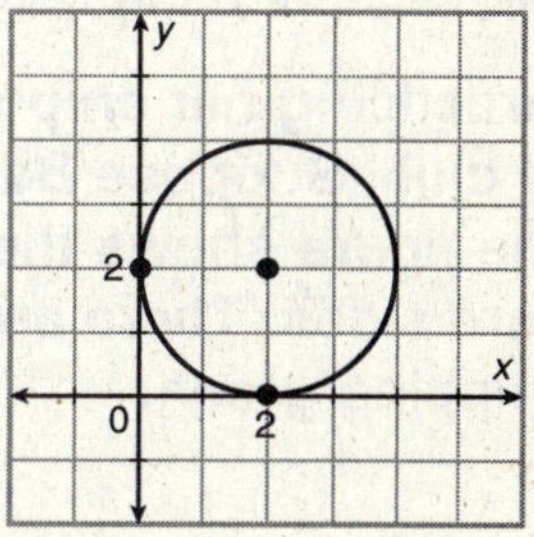

7. The radius of a circle with center (2, 2) that passes through (0, 2) is divided by 2.

8. The bases and the height of a trapezoid with base lengths 4 in. and 8 in. and height 8 in. are all multiplied by $\frac{1}{8}$.

9. A rhombus has an area of 9 cm^2. The area is multiplied by 5. Describe the effects on the diagonals of the rhombus.

10. A circle has a circumference of 14π ft. The area is halved. Describe the effects on the circumference of the circle.

Name ________________________ Date ____________ Class ____________

LESSON 9-6

Practice B
Geometric Probability

A point is randomly chosen on $\overline{AD}$. Find the fractional probability of each event.

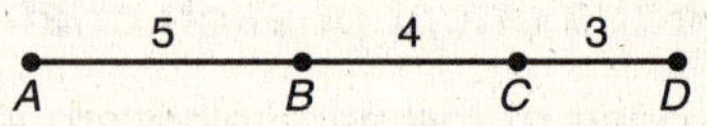

1. The point is on $\overline{AB}$. ____________
2. The point is on $\overline{BD}$. ____________
3. The point is on $\overline{AD}$. ____________
4. The point is not on $\overline{BC}$. ____________

Use the spinner to find the fractional probability of each event.

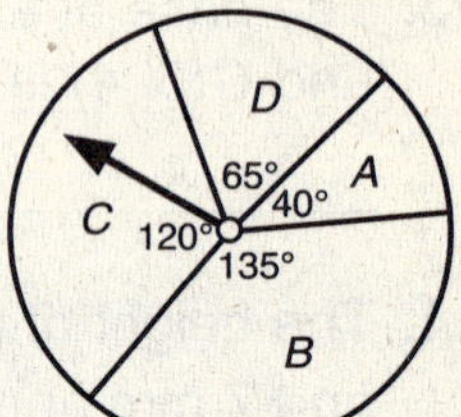

5. the pointer landing in region *C* ____________
6. the pointer landing in region *A* ____________
7. the pointer not landing in region *D* ____________
8. the pointer landing in regions *A* or *B* ____________

Find the probability that a point chosen randomly inside the rectangle is in each given shape. Round answers to the nearest hundredth.

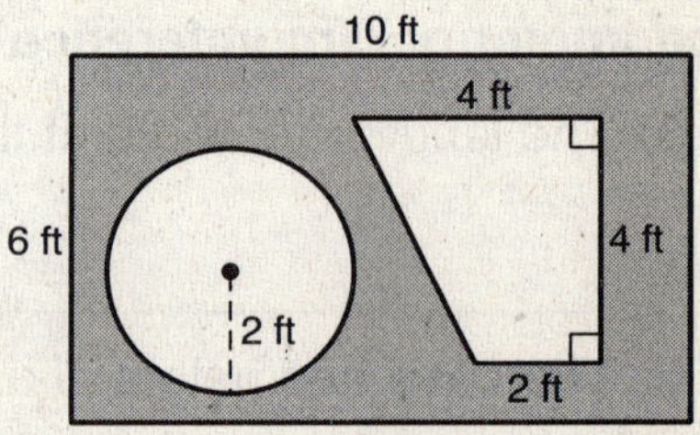

9. the circle ____________
10. the trapezoid ____________
11. the circle or the trapezoid ____________
12. not the circle and the trapezoid ____________

Barb is practicing her chip shots on the chipping green at the local golf club. Suppose Barb's ball drops randomly on the chipping green. The figure shows the chipping green in a grid whose squares have 1-yard sides. There are 18 different 4.5-inch diameter holes on the chipping green.

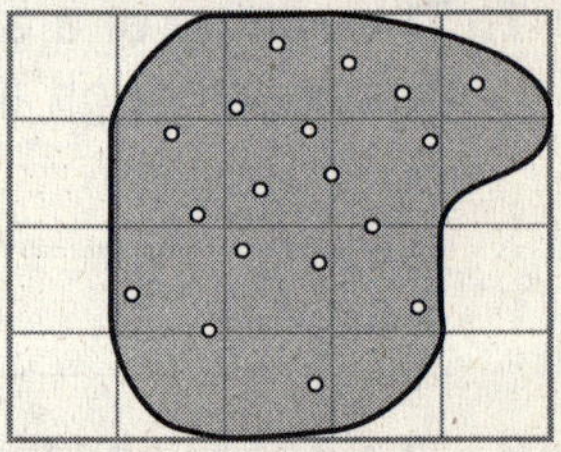

13. Estimate the probability that Barb will chip her ball into any hole. Round to the nearest thousandth. ____________
14. Estimate the probability that Barb will chip her ball into the one hole she is aiming for. Round to the nearest thousandth. ____________
15. Estimate how many chip shots Barb will have to take to ensure that one goes into a randomly selected hole. ____________
16. Barb is getting frustrated, so her shots are even worse. Now the ball drops randomly anywhere in the grid shown in the figure. Estimate the probability that Barb will miss the chipping green. Round to the nearest thousandth. ____________

Name ____________________ Date __________ Class __________

LESSON 10-1

Practice B

Solid Geometry

Classify each figure. Name the vertices, edges, and bases.

1.
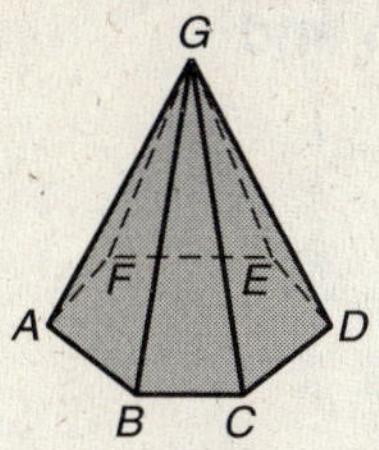

2.
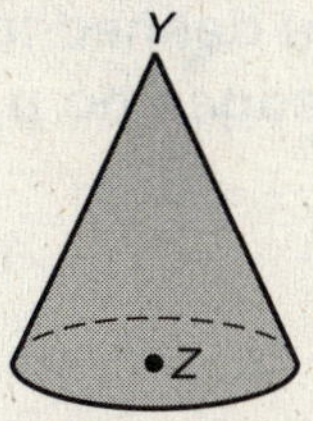

Name the type of solid each object is and sketch an example.

3. a shoe box

4. a can of tuna

Describe the three-dimensional figure that can be made from the given net.

5.
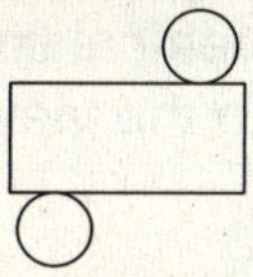

6.
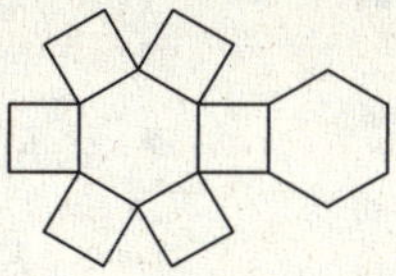

7. Two of the nets below make the same solid. Tell which one does not. ____________

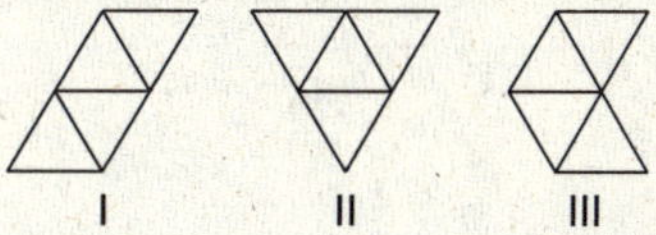

Describe each cross section.

8.
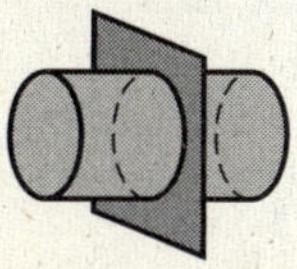

9.
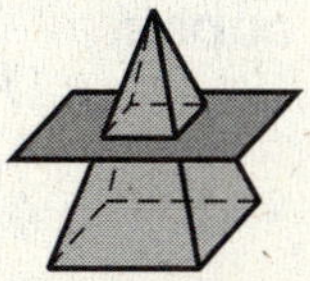

10. After completing Exercises 8 and 9, Lloyd makes a conjecture about the shape of any cross section parallel to the base of a solid. Write your own conjecture.

Name ______________________________________ Date ___________ Class ___________

LESSON 10-2

Practice B

Representations of Three-Dimensional Figures

Draw all six orthographic views of each object. Assume there are no hidden cubes. In your answers, use a dashed line to show that the edges touch and a solid line to show that the edges do not touch.

1. 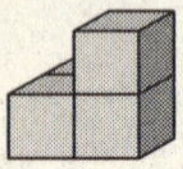

2. 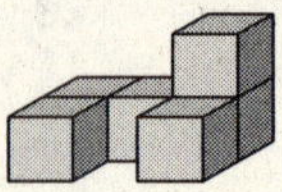

3. Draw an isometric view of the object in Exercise 1.

4. Draw an isometric view of the object in Exercise 2.

5. Draw a block letter T in one-point perspective.

6. Draw a block letter T in two-point perspective. (*Hint:* Draw the vertical line segment that will be closest to the viewer first.)

Determine whether each drawing represents the object at right. Assume there are no hidden cubes.

7. 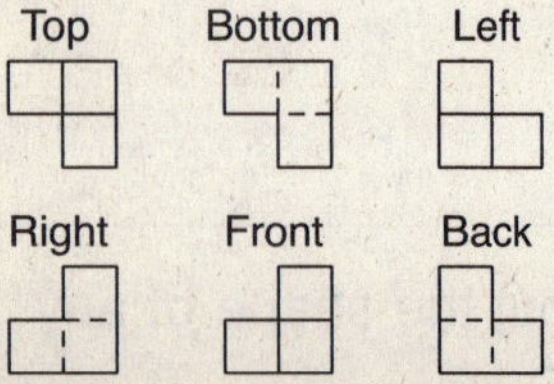

____

8. 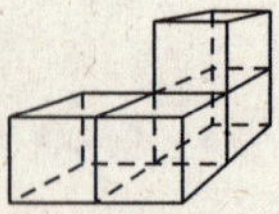

____

Name ______________________ Date ____________ Class ____________

LESSON 10-3

Practice B
Formulas in Three Dimensions

Find the number of vertices, edges, and faces of each polyhedron. Use your results to verify Euler's Formula.

1.

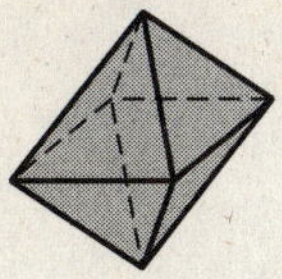

____

____

2.

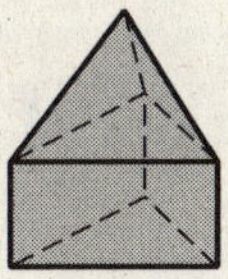

____

____

Find the unknown dimension in each polyhedron. Round to the nearest tenth.

3. the edge length of a cube with a diagonal of 9 ft ____________

4. the length of a diagonal of a 15-mm-by-20-mm-by-8-mm rectangular prism ____________

5. the length of a rectangular prism with width 2 in., height 18 in., and a 21-in. diagonal ____________

Graph each figure.

6. a square prism with base edge length 4 units, height 2 units, and one vertex at (0, 0, 0)

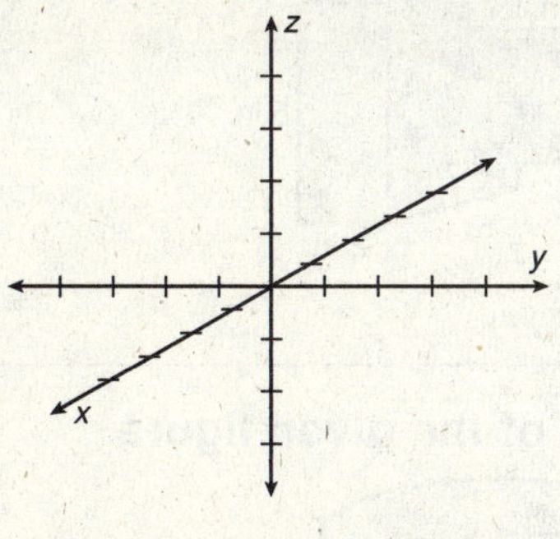

7. a cone with base diameter 6 units, height 3 units, and base centered at (0, 0, 0)

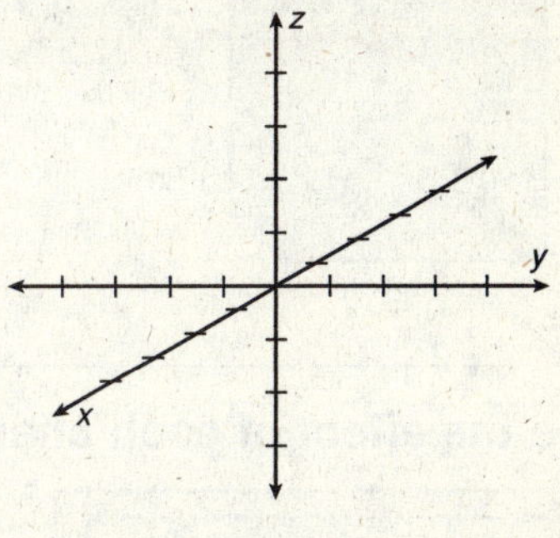

Find the distance between the given points. Find the midpoint of the segment with the given endpoints. Round to the nearest tenth if necessary.

8. (1, 10, 3) and (5, 5, 5)

____

9. (−8, 0, 11) and (2, −6, −17)

____

Name ______________________ Date ____________ Class ____________

LESSON **10-4**

Practice B

Surface Area of Prisms and Cylinders

Find the lateral area and surface area of each right prism. Round to the nearest tenth if necessary.

1. 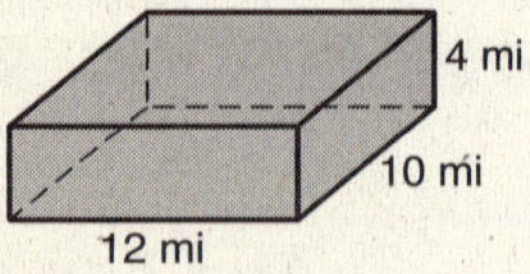

the rectangular prism

____

2. 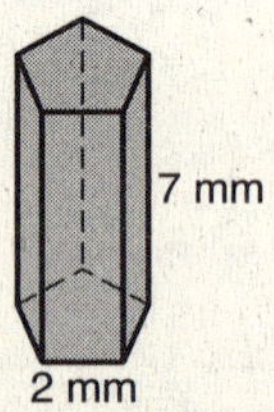

the regular pentagonal prism

____

3. a cube with edge length 20 inches ______________________

Find the lateral area and surface area of each right cylinder. Give your answers in terms of π.

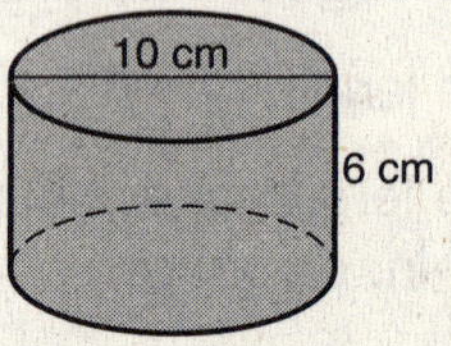

4. ______________________

5. a cylinder with base area 169π ft^2 and a height twice the radius ______________________

6. a cylinder with base circumference 8π m and a height one-fourth the radius ______________________

Find the surface area of each composite figure. Round to the nearest tenth.

7. 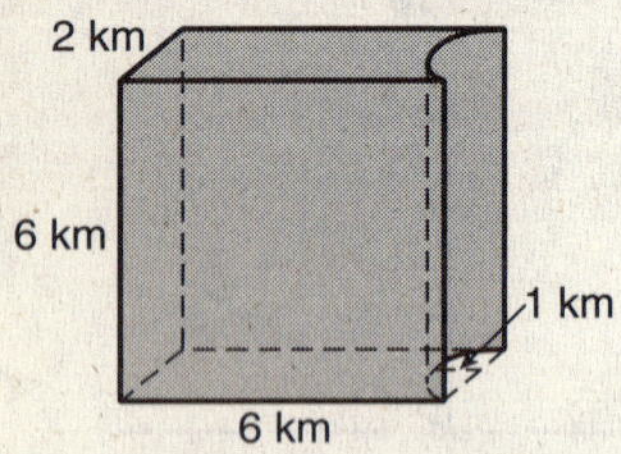

____

8. 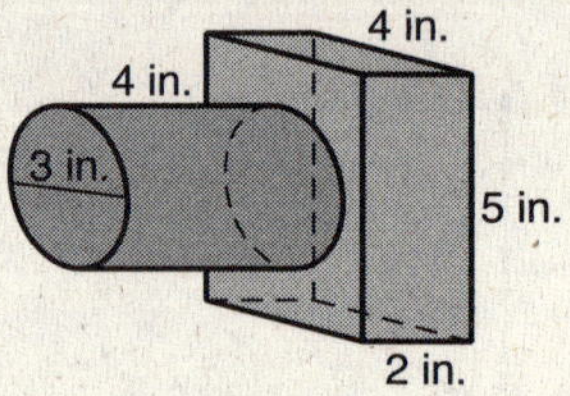

____

Describe the effect of each change on the surface area of the given figure.

9. 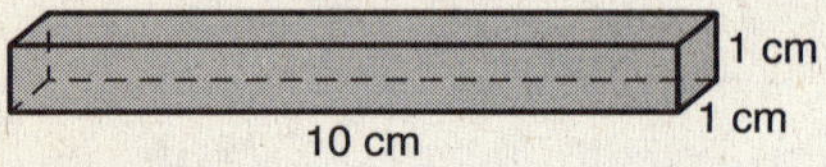

The dimensions are multiplied by 12.

____

10. 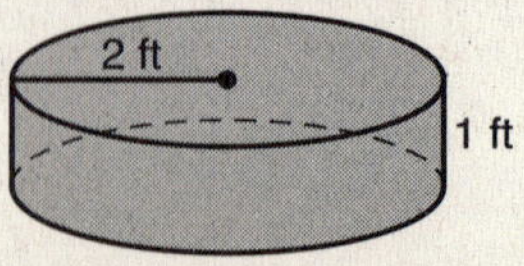

The dimensions are divided by 4.

____

Toby has eight cubes with edge length 1 inch. He can stack the cubes into three different rectangular prisms: 2-by-2-by-2, 8-by-1-by-1, and 2-by-4-by-1. Each prism has a volume of 8 cubic inches.

11. Tell which prism has the smallest surface-area-to-volume ratio. ______________________

12. Tell which prism has the greatest surface-area-to-volume ratio. ______________________

Name ______________________ Date __________ Class __________

LESSON **10-5**

Practice B

Surface Area of Pyramids and Cones

Find the lateral area and surface area of each regular right solid. Round to the nearest tenth if necessary.

1. 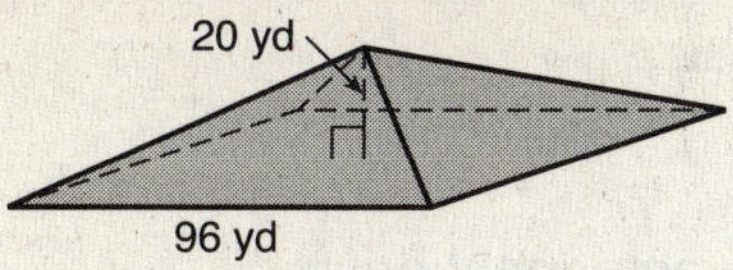

2. 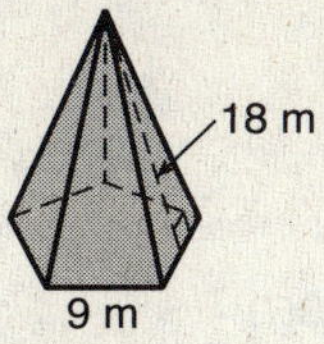

3. a regular hexagonal pyramid with base edge length 12 mi and slant height 15 mi

Find the lateral area and surface area of each right cone. Give your answers in terms of π.

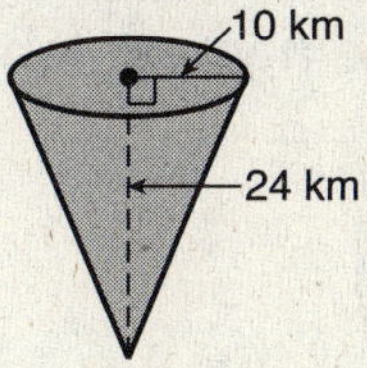

4. ______________________

5. a right cone with base circumference 14π ft and slant height 3 times the radius

6. a right cone with diameter 240 cm and altitude 35 cm

Describe the effect of each change on the surface area of the given figure.

7. 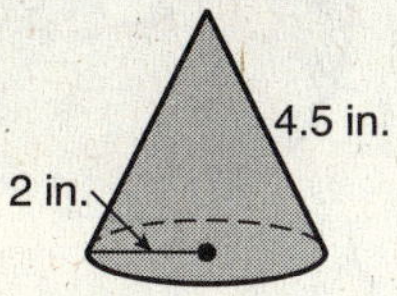

The dimensions are multiplied by $\frac{1}{5}$.

8. 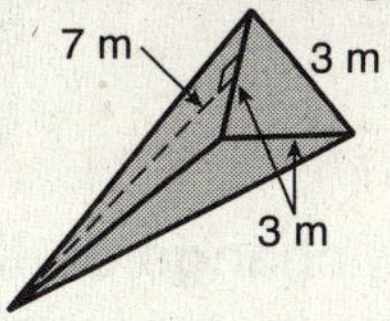

The dimensions are multiplied by $\frac{3}{2}$.

Find the surface area of each composite figure. Round to the nearest tenth if necessary.

9. 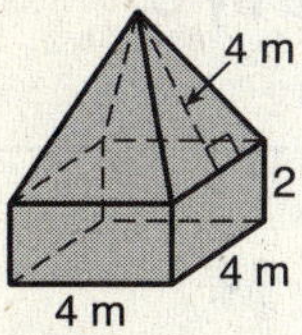

10. 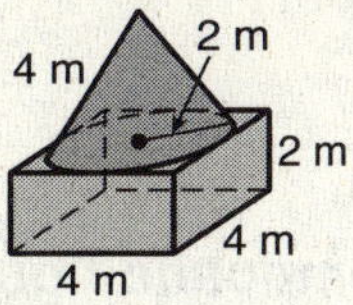

11. The water cooler at Mohammed's office has small conical paper cups for drinking. He uncurls one of the cups and measures the paper. Based on the diagram of the uncurled cup, find the diameter of the cone.

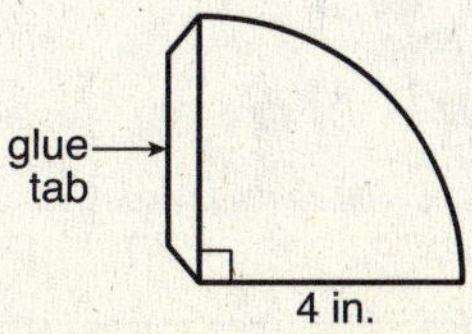

Name ______________________ Date __________ Class __________

LESSON 10-6

Practice B

Volume of Prisms and Cylinders

Find the volume of each prism. Round to the nearest tenth if necessary.

1. 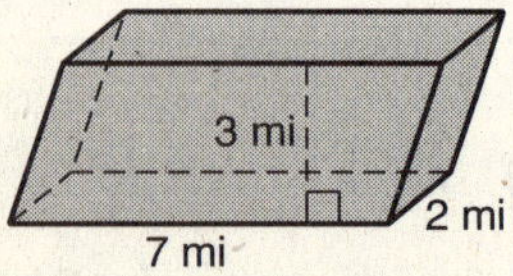

the oblique rectangular prism

____

2. 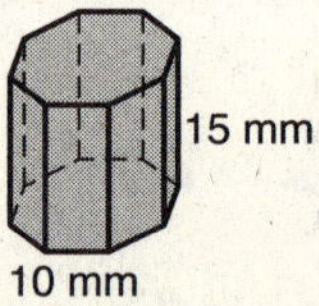

the regular octagonal prism

____

3. a cube with edge length 0.75 m ________________________

Find the volume of each cylinder. Give your answers both in terms of π and rounded to the nearest tenth.

4. 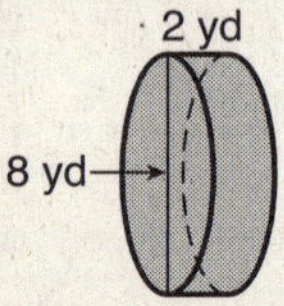

____

5. 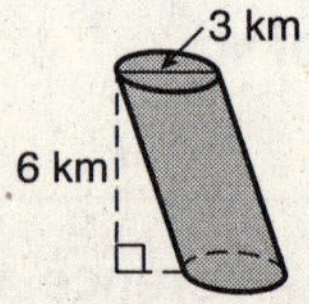

____

6. a cylinder with base circumference 18π ft and height 10 ft ________________________

7. CDs have the dimensions shown in the figure. Each CD is 1 mm thick. Find the volume in cubic centimeters of a stack of 25 CDs. Round to the nearest tenth.

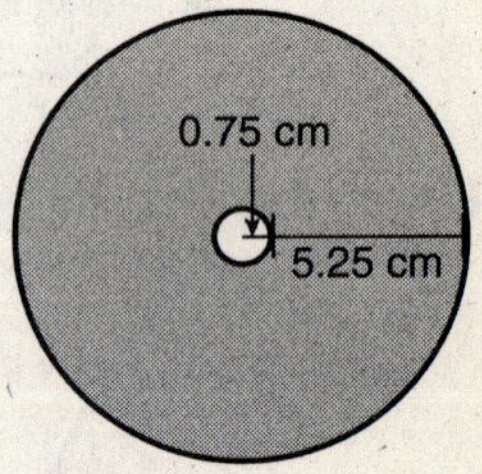

____

Describe the effect of each change on the volume of the given figure.

8. 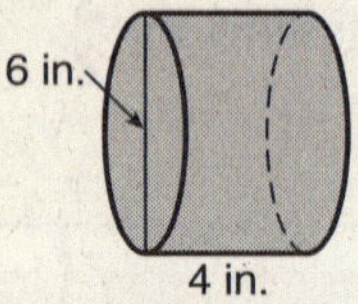

The dimensions are halved.

____

9. 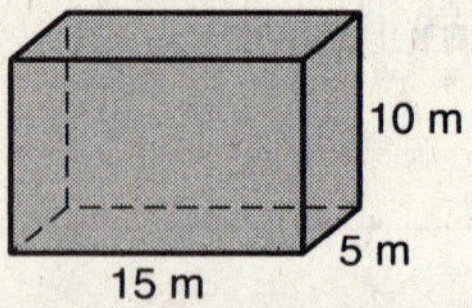

The dimensions are divided by 5.

____

Find the volume of each composite figure. Round to the nearest tenth.

10. 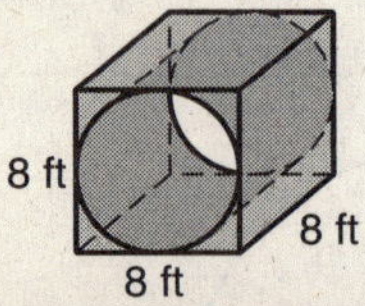

____

11. 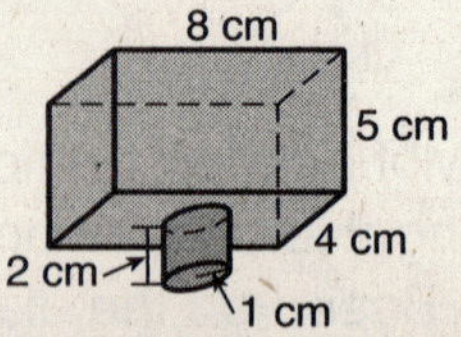

____

Name ______________________ Date __________ Class __________

LESSON 10-7

Practice B

Volume of Pyramids and Cones

Find the volume of each pyramid. Round to the nearest tenth if necessary.

1.

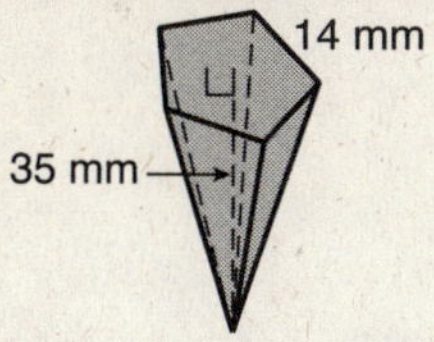

the regular pentagonal pyramid

____

2.

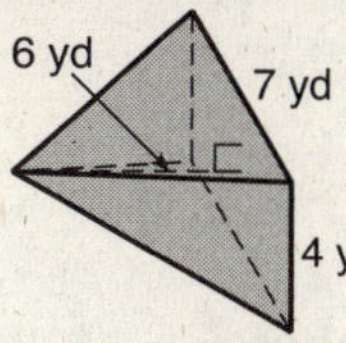

the rectangular right pyramid

____

3. Giza in Egypt is the site of the three great Egyptian pyramids. Each pyramid has a square base. The largest pyramid was built for Khufu. When first built, it had base edges of 754 feet and a height of 481 feet. Over the centuries, some of the stone eroded away and some was taken for newer buildings. Khufu's pyramid today has base edges of 745 feet and a height of 471 feet. To the nearest cubic foot, find the difference between the original and current volumes of the pyramid.

____

Find the volume of each cone. Give your answers both in terms of π and rounded to the nearest tenth.

4.

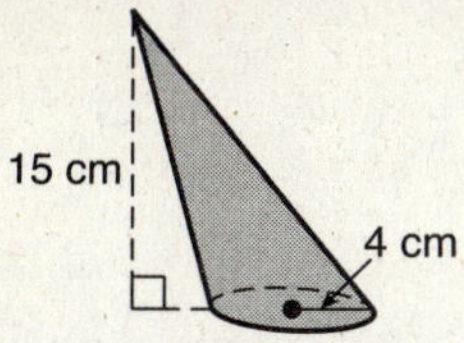

____

5.

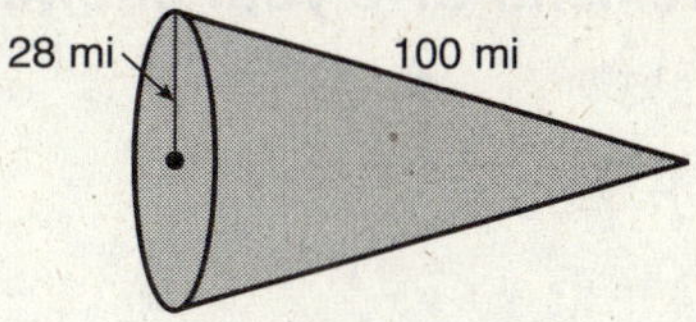

____

6. a cone with base circumference 6π m and a height equal to half the radius

____

7. Compare the volume of a cone and the volume of a cylinder with equal height and base area.

____

Describe the effect of each change on the volume of the given figure.

8.

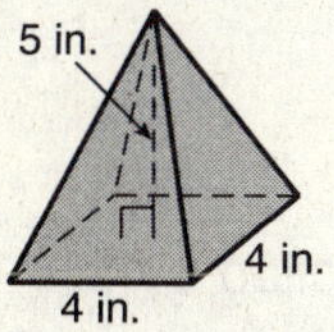

The dimensions are multiplied by $\frac{2}{3}$.

____

9.

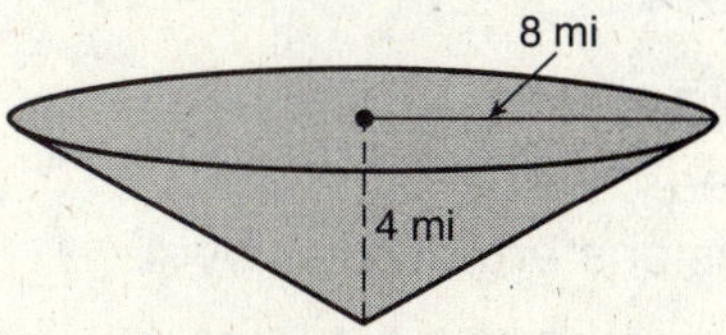

The dimensions are tripled.

____

Find the volume of each composite figure. Round to the nearest tenth.

10.

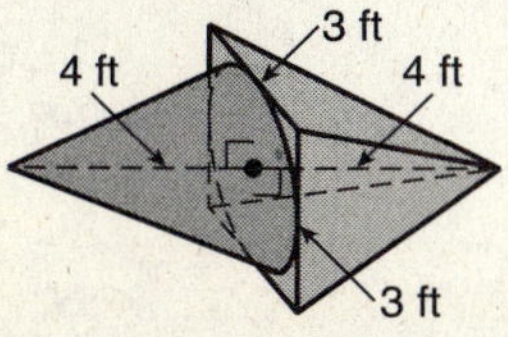

____

11.

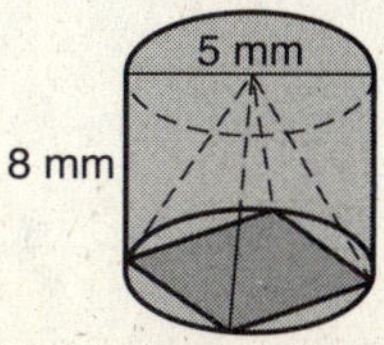

____

Name ____________________ Date __________ Class __________

LESSON 10-8

Practice B
Spheres

Find each measurement. Give your answers in terms of π.

1.
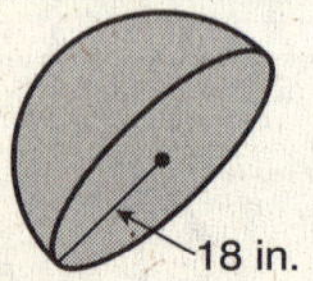

the volume of the hemisphere

____

2.
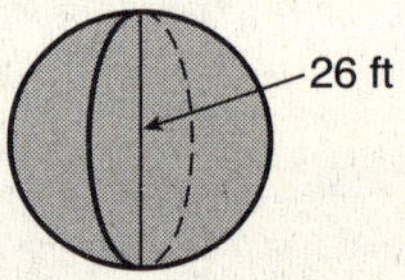

the volume of the sphere

____

3. the diameter of a sphere with volume $\frac{500\pi}{3}$ m^3 ________________________

4. The figure shows a grapefruit half. The radius to the outside of the rind is 5 cm. The radius to the inside of the rind is 4 cm. The edible part of the grapefruit is divided into 12 equal sections. Find the volume of the half grapefruit and the volume of one edible section. Give your answers in terms of π.

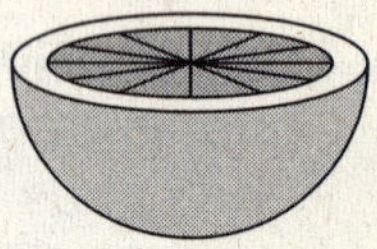

____

Find each measurement. Give your answers in terms of π.

5.
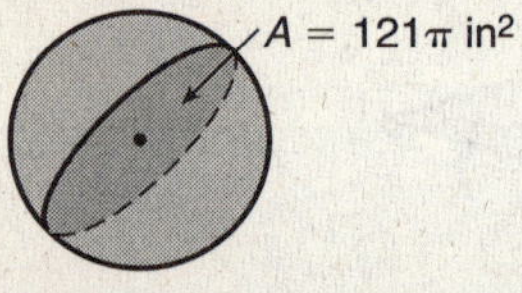

the surface area of the sphere

____

6.
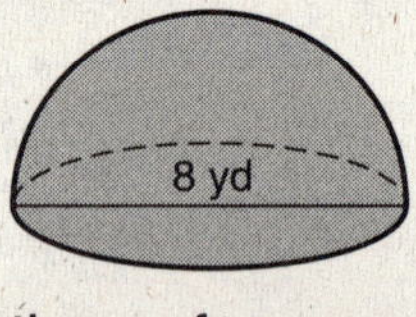

the surface area of the closed hemisphere and its circular base

____

7. the volume of a sphere with surface area 196π km^2 ________________________

Describe the effect of each change on the given measurement of the figure.

8.
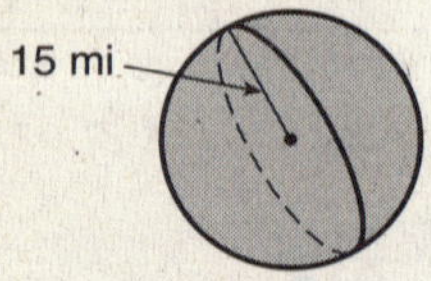

surface area
The dimensions are divided by 4.

____

9.
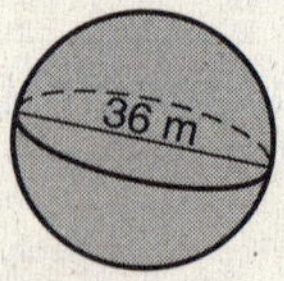

volume
The dimensions are multiplied by $\frac{2}{5}$.

____

Find the surface area and volume of each composite figure. Round to the nearest tenth.

10.
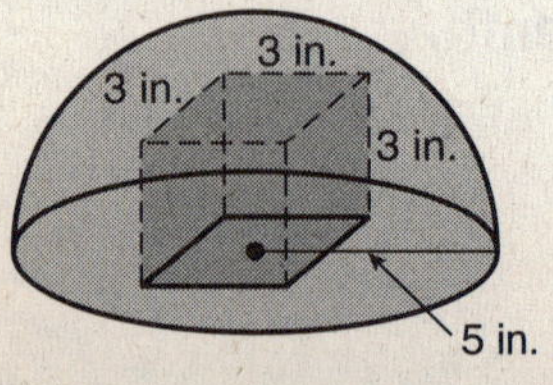

____

11.
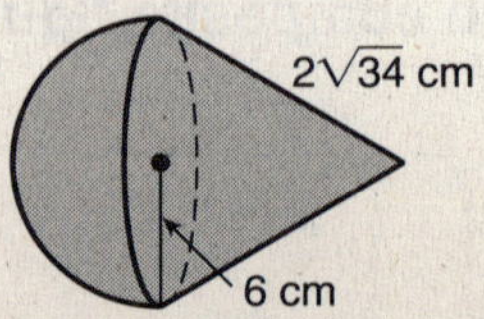

____

Name ______________________ Date ____________ Class ____________

LESSON 11-1

Practice B

Lines That Intersect Circles

Identify each line or segment that intersects each circle.

1. 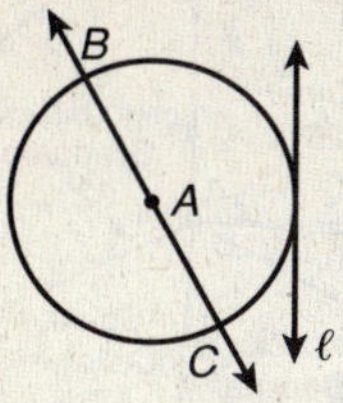

____

____

2. 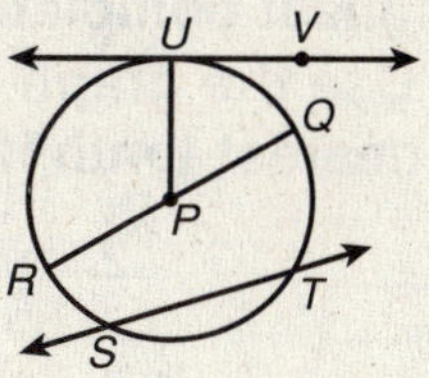

____

____

Find the length of each radius. Identify the point of tangency and write the equation of the tangent line at this point.

3. 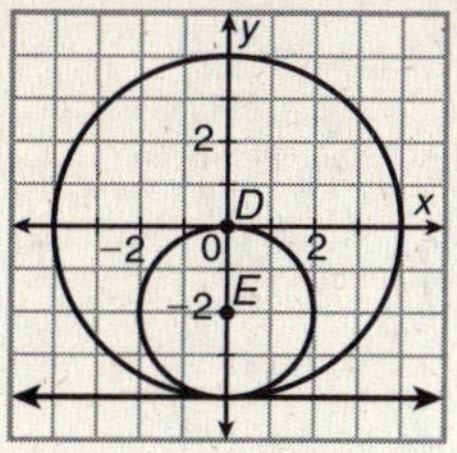

____

____

____

4. 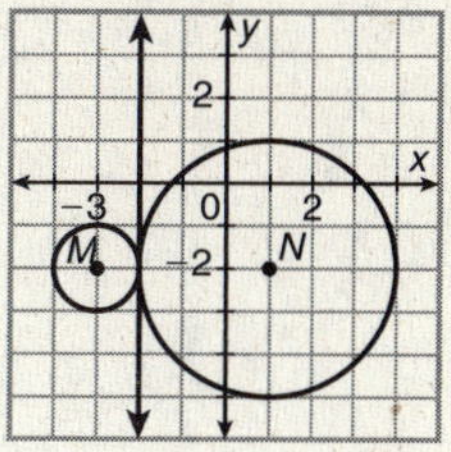

____

____

____

5. The Moon's orbit is not exactly circular, but the average distance from its surface to Earth's surface is 384,000 kilometers. The diameter of the Moon is 3476 kilometers. Find the distance from the surface of Earth to the visible edge of the Moon if the Moon is directly above the observer. Round to the nearest kilometer. (*Note:* The figure is not drawn to scale.)

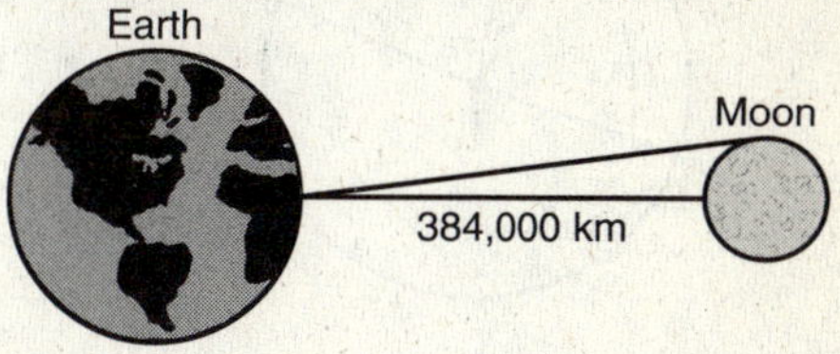

____

In Exercises 6 and 7, $\overline{EF}$ and $\overline{EG}$ are tangent to ⊙*H*. Find *EF*.

6. 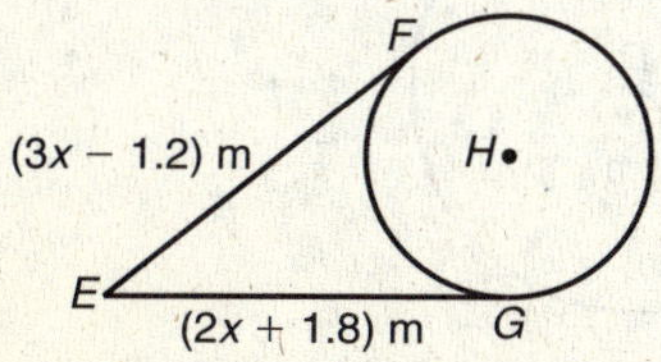

____

7. 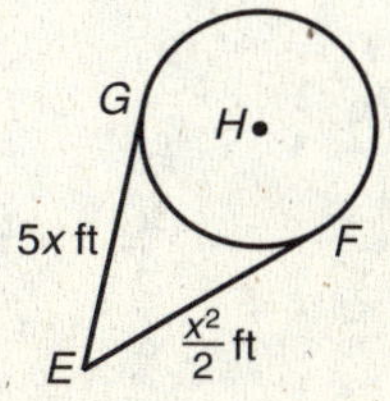

____

Name ________________________ Date ____________ Class ____________

LESSON 11-2

Practice B

Arcs and Chords

The circle graph shows data collected by the U.S. Census Bureau in 2004 on the highest completed educational level for people 25 and older. Use the graph to find each of the following. Round to the nearest tenth if necessary.

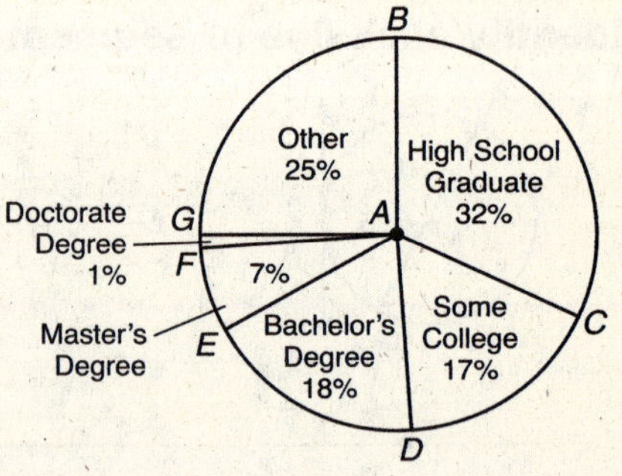

1. m∠*CAB* ____________ 2. m∠*DAG* ____________

3. m∠*EAC* ____________ 4. m$\overarc{BG}$ ____________

5. m$\overarc{GF}$ ____________ 6. m$\overarc{BDE}$ ____________

Find each measure.

7.

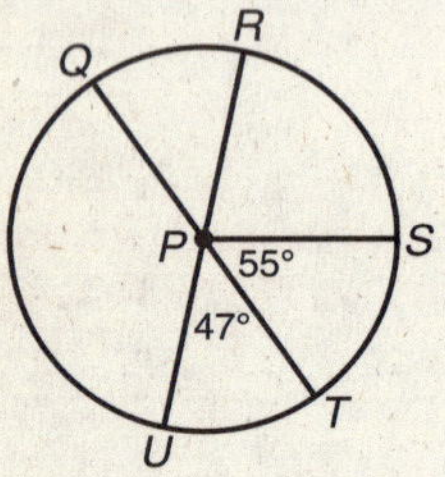

m$\overarc{QS}$ ____________

m$\overarc{RQT}$ ____________

8.

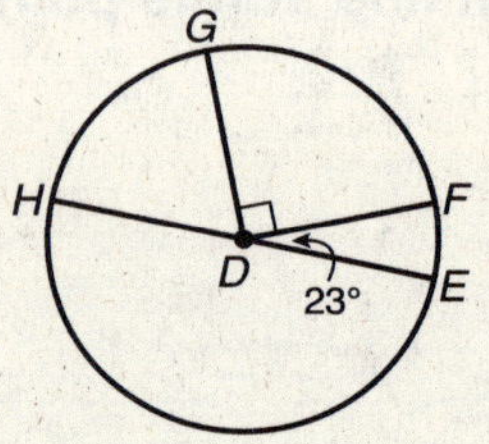

m$\overarc{HG}$ ____________

m$\overarc{FEH}$ ____________

9.

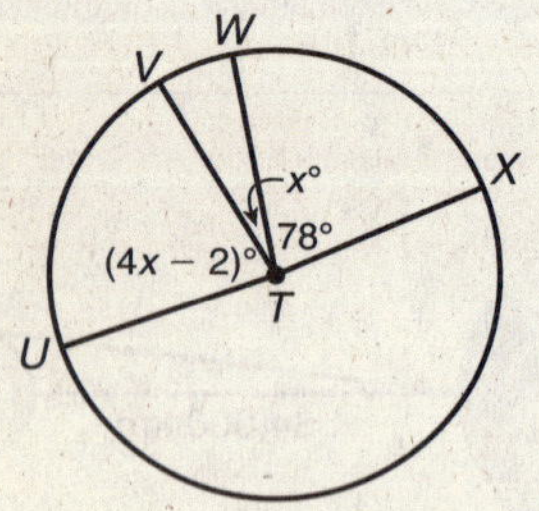

Find m∠*UTW*. ____________

10.

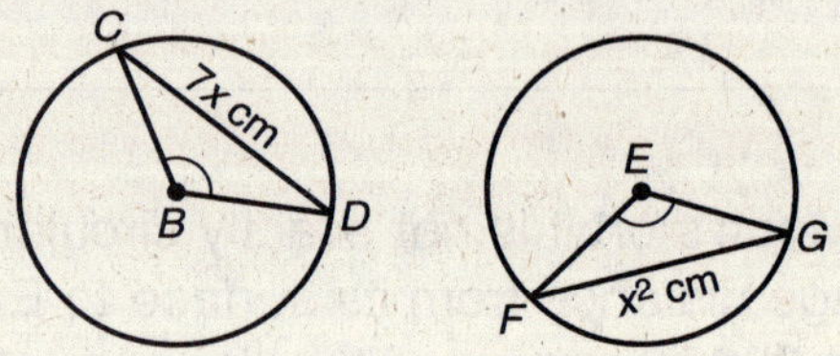

⊙*B* ≅ ⊙*E*, and ∠*CBD* ≅ ∠*FEG*.

Find *FG*. ____________

Find each length. Round to the nearest tenth.

11.

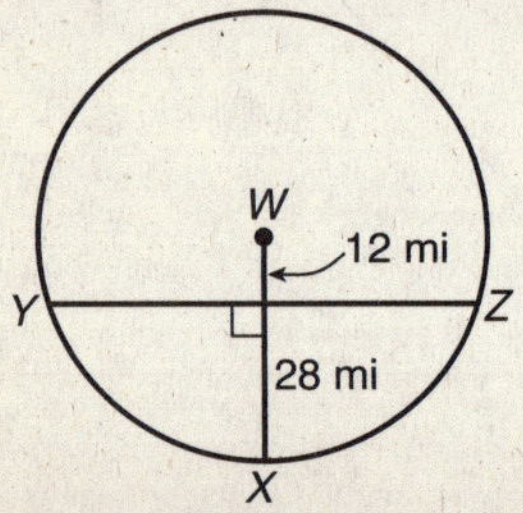

ZY ____________________________

12.

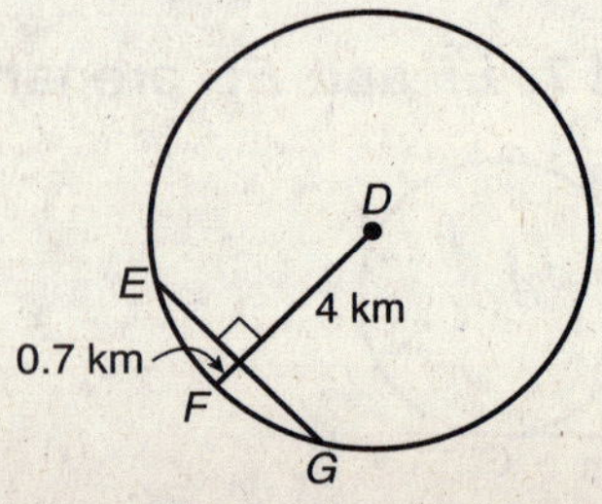

EG ____________________________

Name ______________________ Date ____________ Class ____________

LESSON 11-3

Practice B

Sector Area and Arc Length

Find the area of each sector. Give your answer in terms of π and rounded to the nearest hundredth.

1.

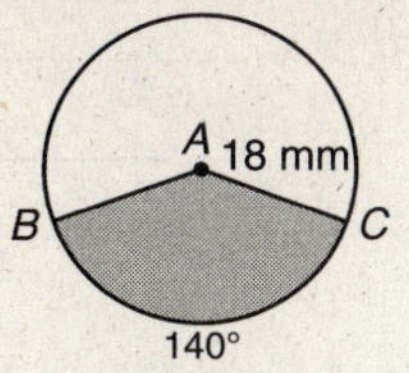

sector *BAC* ______________________

2.

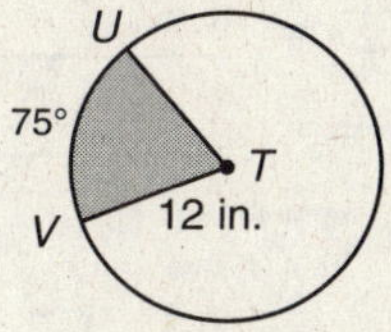

sector *UTV* ______________________

3.

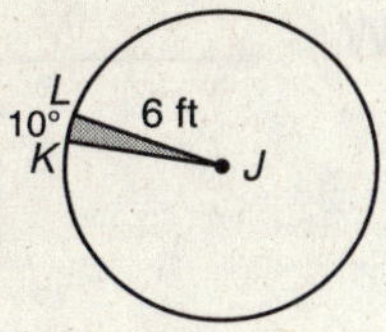

sector *KJL* ______________________

4.

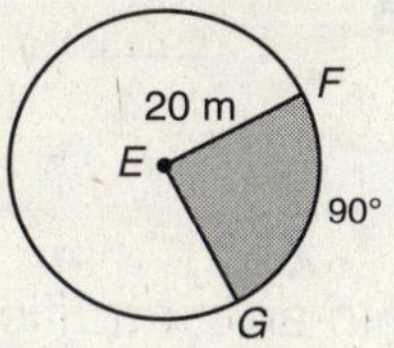

sector *FEG* ______________________

5. The speedometer needle in Ignacio's car is 2 inches long. The needle sweeps out a 130° sector during acceleration from 0 to 60 mi/h. Find the area of this sector. Round to the nearest hundredth. ______________

Find the area of each segment to the nearest hundredth.

6.

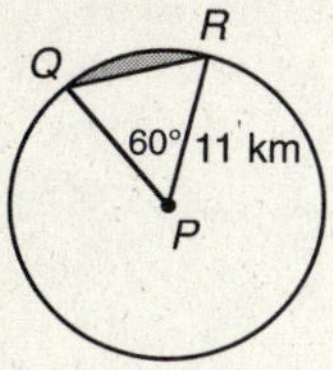

____

7.

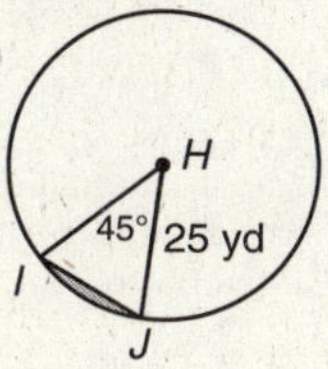

____

8.

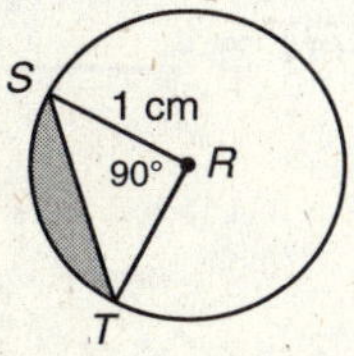

____

9.

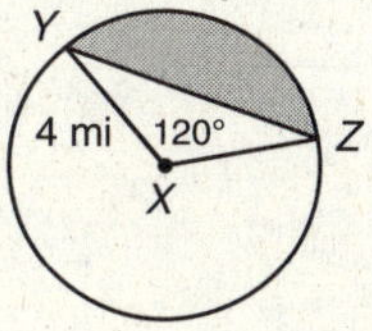

____

Find each arc length. Give your answer in terms of π and rounded to the nearest hundredth.

10.

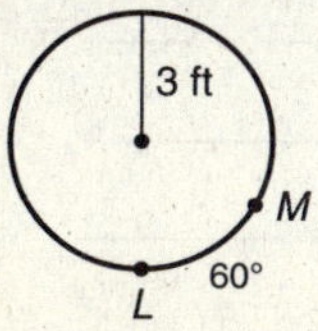

____

11.

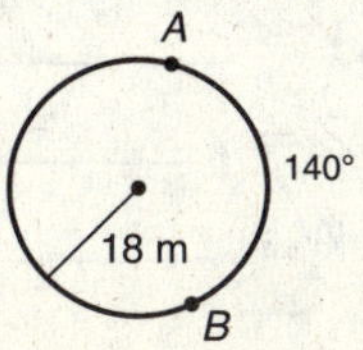

____

12. an arc with measure 45° in a circle with radius 2 mi ______________

13. an arc with measure 120° in a circle with radius 15 mm ______________

Name ______________________________ Date ____________ Class ____________

LESSON **11-4**

Practice B

Inscribed Angles

Find each measure.

1. 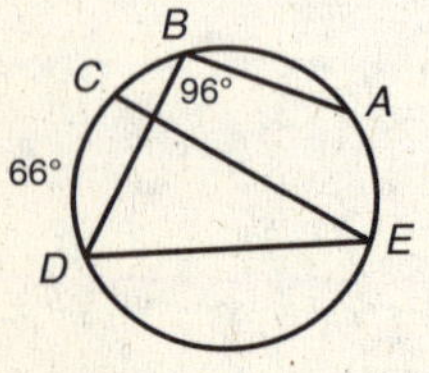

m∠CED = ________

m$\widehat{DEA}$ = ________

2. 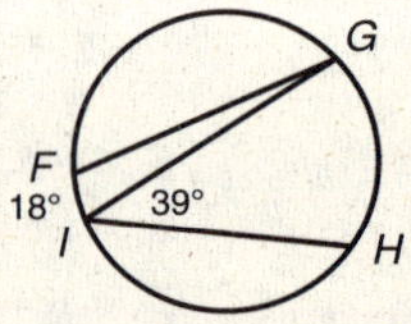

m∠FGI = ________

m$\widehat{GH}$ = ________

3. 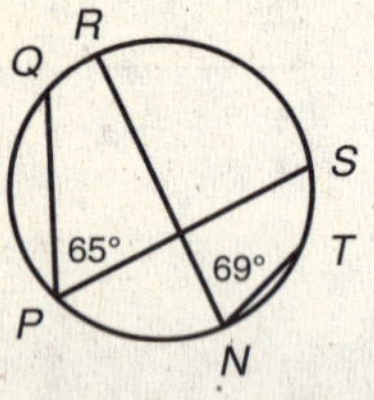

m$\widehat{QRS}$ = ________

m$\widehat{TSR}$ = ________

4. 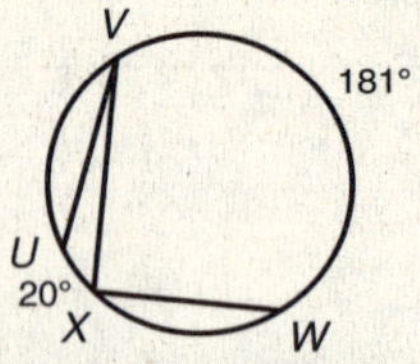

m∠XVU = ________

m∠VXW = ________

5. A circular radar screen in an air traffic control tower shows these flight paths. Find m∠LNK. ________

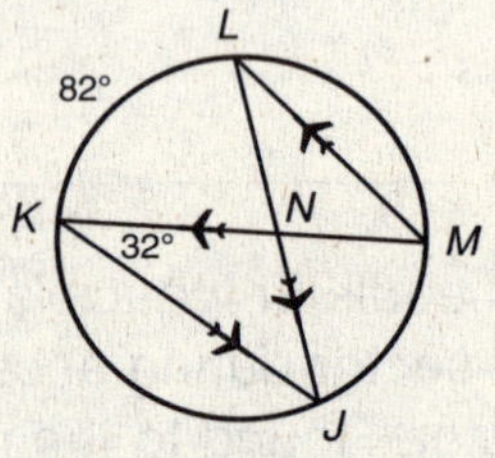

Find each value.

6. 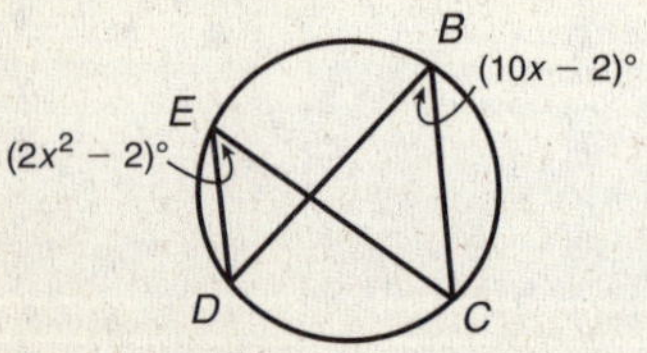

m∠CED = ________

7. 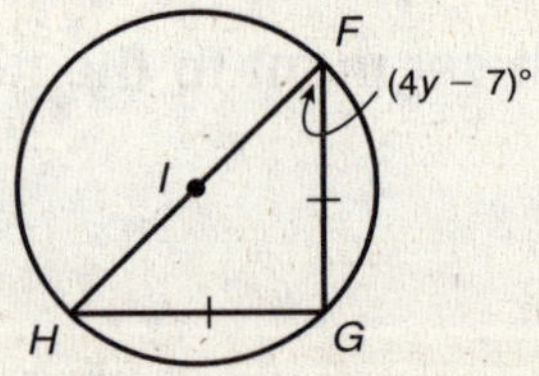

y = ________

8. 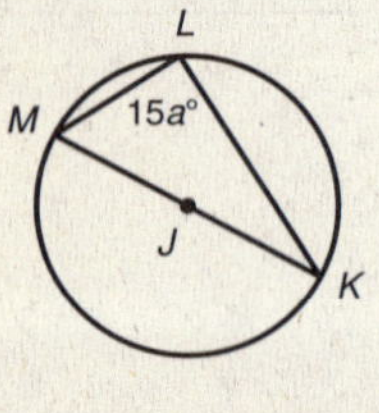

a = ________

9. 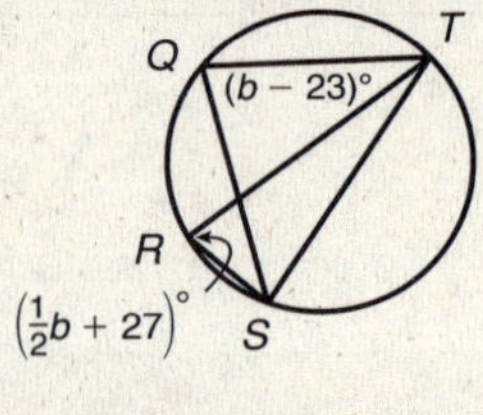

m∠SRT = ________

Find the angle measures of each inscribed quadrilateral.

10. 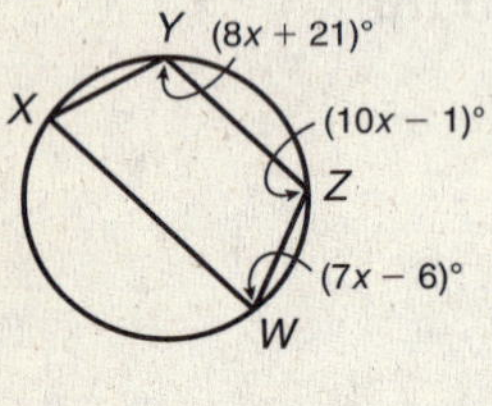

m∠X = ________

m∠Y = ________

m∠Z = ________

m∠W = ________

11. 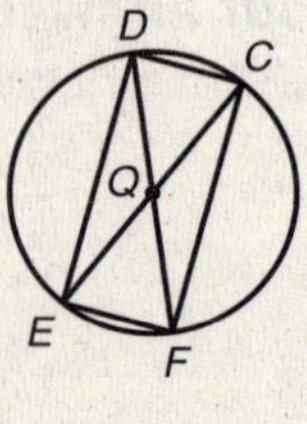

m∠C = ________

m∠D = ________

m∠E = ________

m∠F = ________

12. 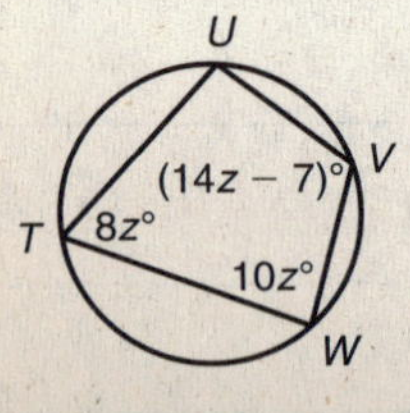

m∠T = ________

m∠U = ________

m∠V = ________

m∠W = ________

13. 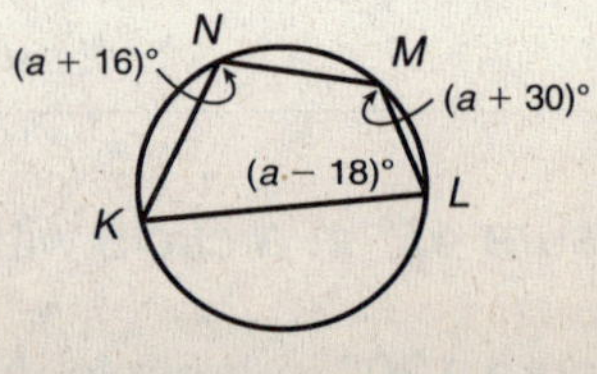

m∠K = ________

m∠L = ________

m∠M = ________

m∠N = ________

Name ______________________________ Date ____________ Class ____________

LESSON 11-5

Practice B

Angle Relationships in Circles

Find each measure.

1. 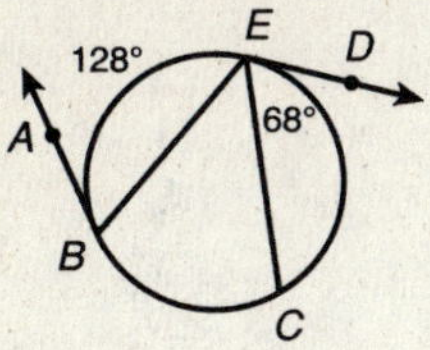

m∠*ABE* = ____________

m$\overparen{BC}$ = ____________

2. 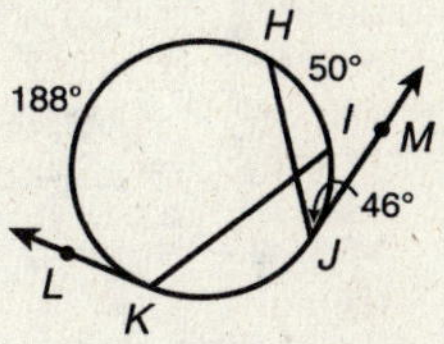

m∠*LKI* = ____________

m$\overparen{IJ}$ = ____________

3. 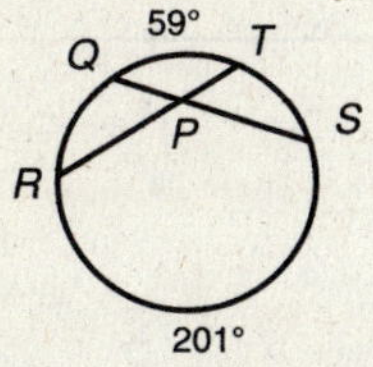

m∠*RPS* = ____________

4. 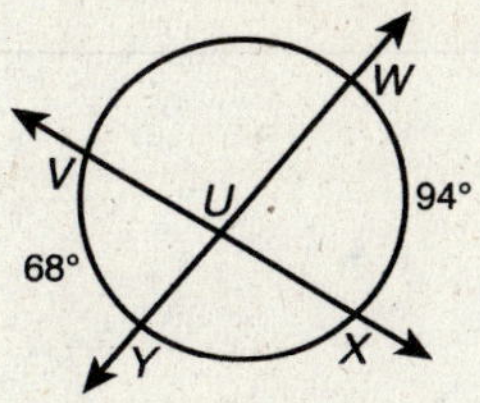

m∠*YUX* = ____________

Find the value of *x*.

5. 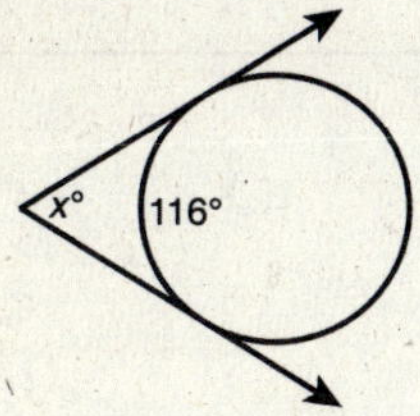

____

6. 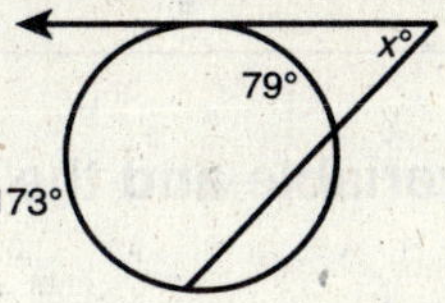

____

7. 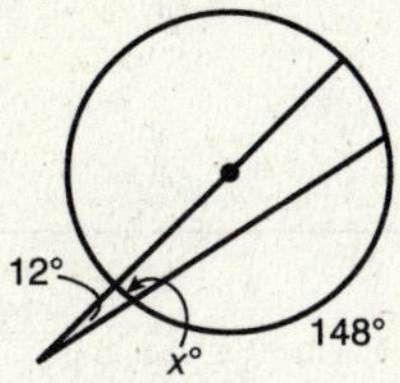

____

8. 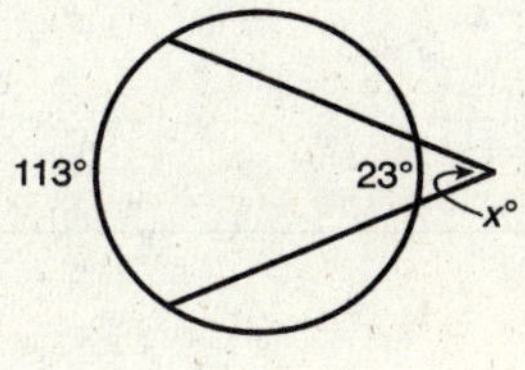

____

9. The figure shows a spinning wheel. The large wheel is turned by hand or with a foot trundle. A belt attaches to a small bobbin that turns very quickly. The bobbin twists raw materials into thread, twine, or yarn. Each pair of spokes intercepts a 30° arc. Find the value of *x*.

____

Find each measure.

10. 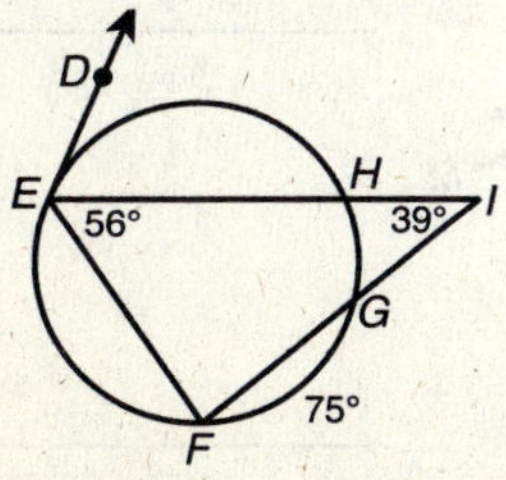

m∠*DEI* = ____________

m$\overparen{EF}$ = ____________

11. 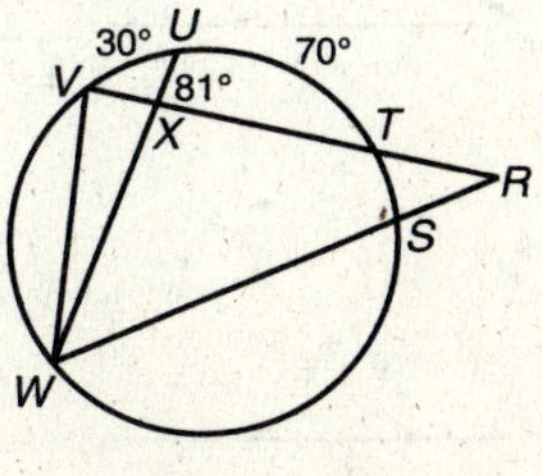

m∠*WVR* = ____________

m$\overparen{TUW}$ = ____________

Name ______________________ Date ___________ Class ___________

LESSON 11-6

Practice B
Segment Relationships in Circles

Find the value of the variable and the length of each chord.

1.

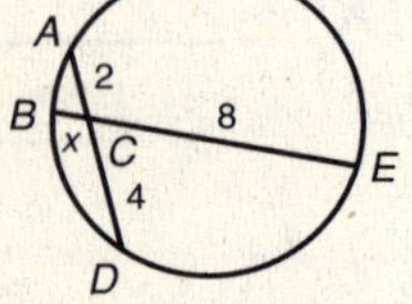

____

2.

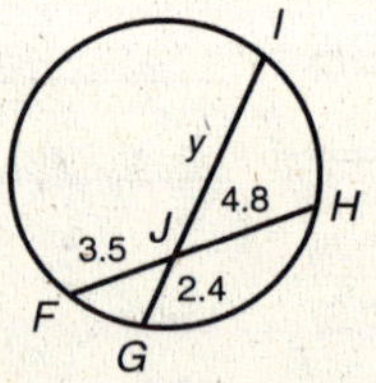

____

3.

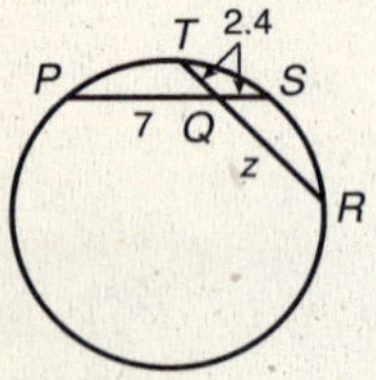

____

4.

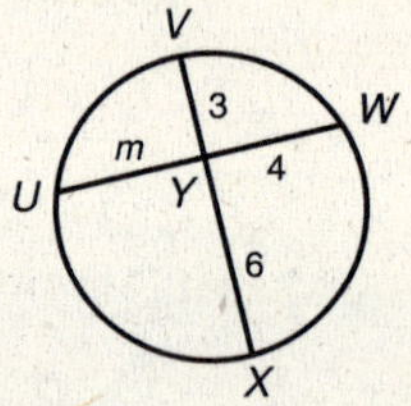

____

Find the value of the variable and the length of each secant segment.

5.

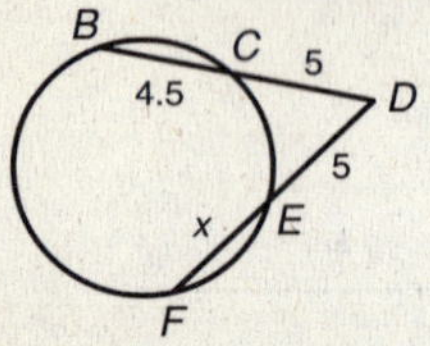

____

6.

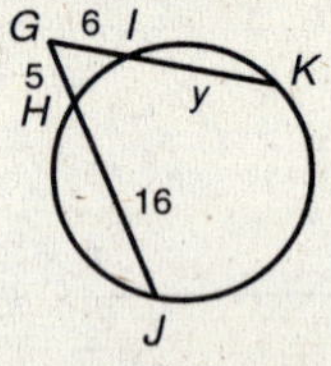

____

7.

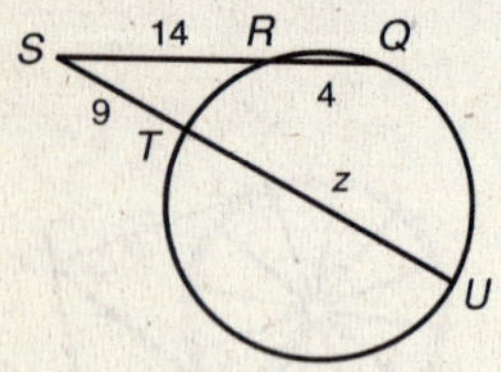

____

8.

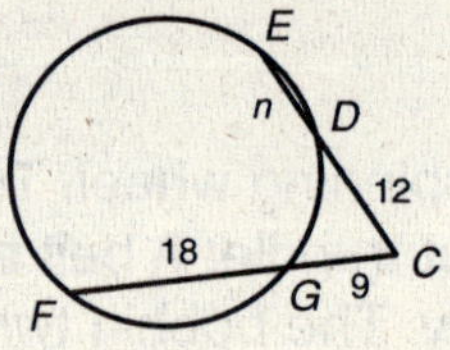

____

Find the value of the variable. Give answers in simplest radical form if necessary.

9.

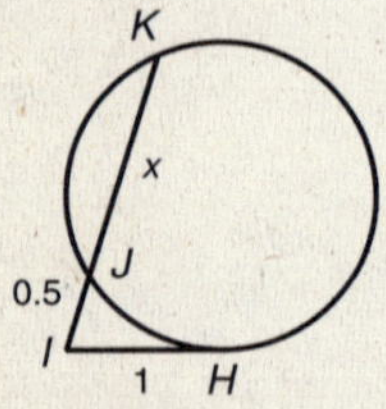

____

10.

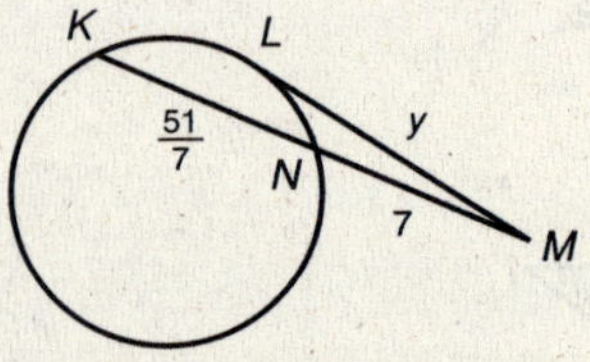

____

11.

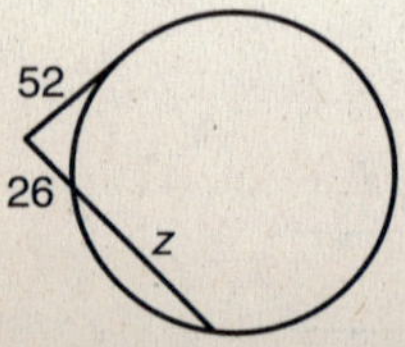

____

12.

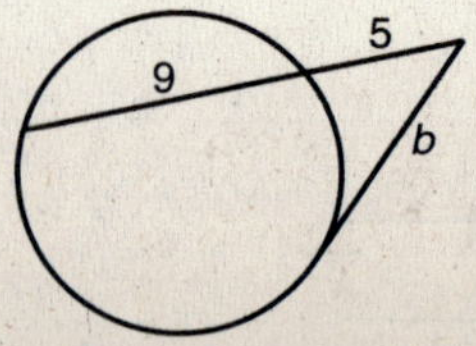

____

Name ______________________ Date ____________ Class ____________

LESSON **11-7**

Practice B

Circles in the Coordinate Plane

Write the equation of each circle.

1. $\odot X$ centered at the origin with radius 10 ____________
2. $\odot R$ with center $R(-1, 8)$ and radius 5 ____________
3. $\odot P$ with center $P(-5, -5)$ and radius $2\sqrt{5}$ ____________
4. $\odot O$ centered at the origin that passes through $(9, -2)$ ____________
5. $\odot B$ with center $B(0, -2)$ that passes through $(-6, 0)$ ____________
6. $\odot F$ with center $F(11, 4)$ that passes through $(-2, 5)$. ____________

Graph each equation.

7. $x^2 + y^2 = 25$

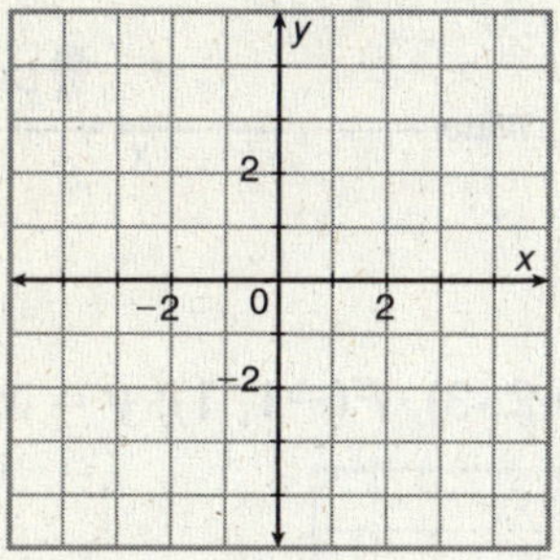

8. $(x + 2)^2 + (y - 1)^2 = 4$

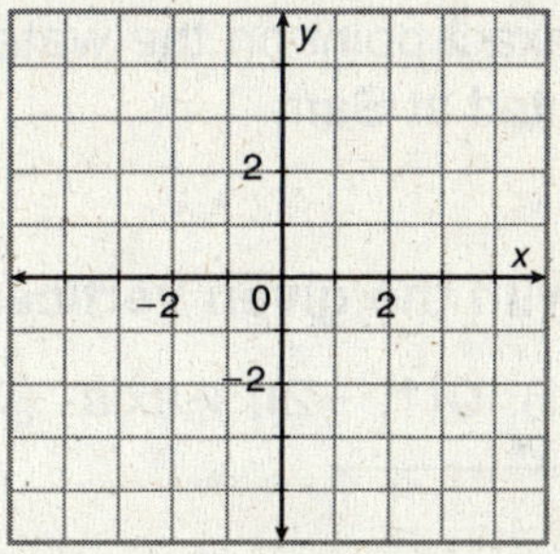

9. $x^2 + (y + 3)^2 = 1$

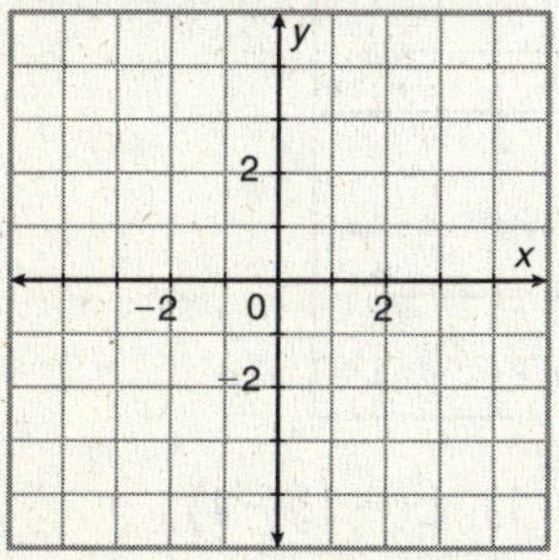

10. $(x - 1)^2 + (y - 1)^2 = 16$

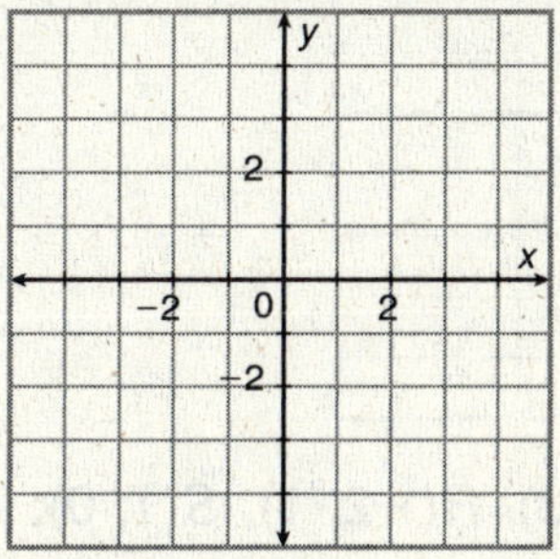

Crater Lake in Oregon is a roughly circular lake. The lake basin formed about 7000 years ago when the top of a volcano exploded in an immense explosion. Hillman Peak, Garfield Peak, and Cloudcap are three mountain peaks on the rim of the lake. The peaks are located in a coordinate plane at $H(-4, 1)$, $G(-2, -3)$, and $C(5, -2)$.

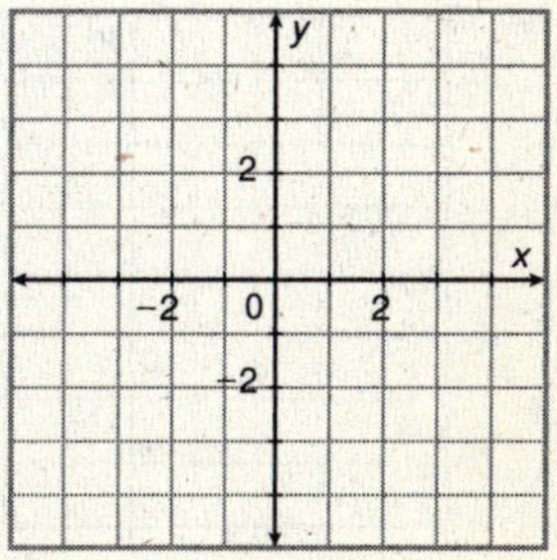

11. Find the coordinates of the center of the lake.

____

12. Each unit of the coordinate plane represents $\frac{3}{5}$ mile. Find the diameter of the lake. ____________

Name ______________________ Date ____________ Class ____________

LESSON 12-1

Practice B
Reflections

Tell whether each transformation appears to be a reflection.

1. 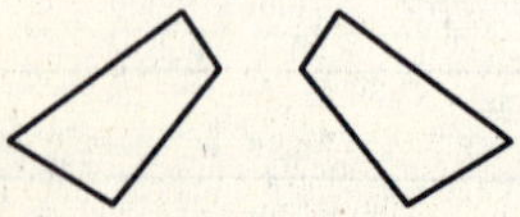 ________

2.  ________

3. 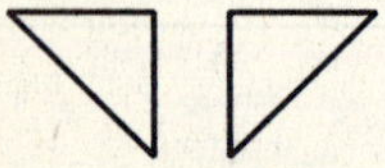 ________

4. 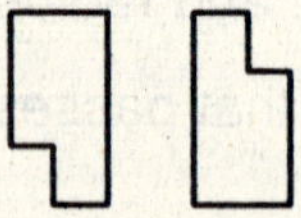 ________

Draw the reflection of each figure across the line.

5. 

6. 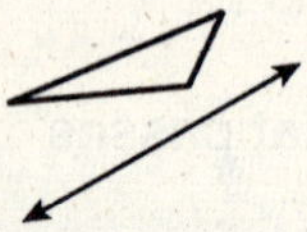

7. Sam is about to dive into a still pool, but some sunlight is reflected off the surface of the water into his eyes. On the figure, plot the exact point on the water's surface where the sunlight is reflected at Sam.

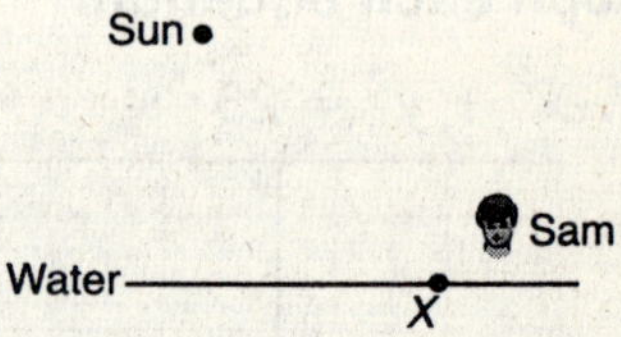

Reflect the figure with the given vertices across the given line.

8. $A(4, 4)$, $B(3, -1)$, $C(1, -2)$; y-axis

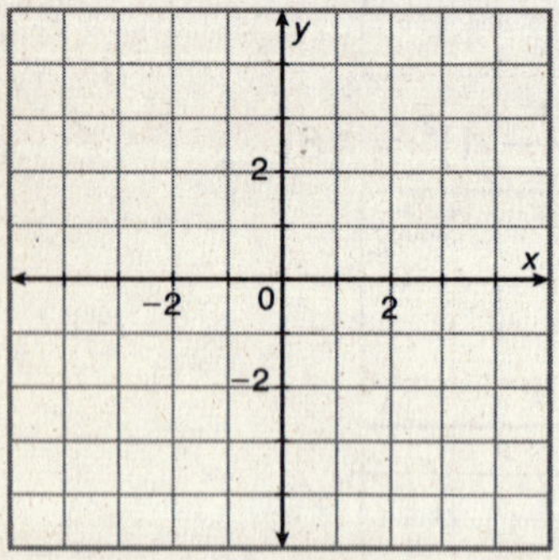

9. $D(-4, -1)$, $E(-2, 3)$, $F(-1, 1)$; $y = x$

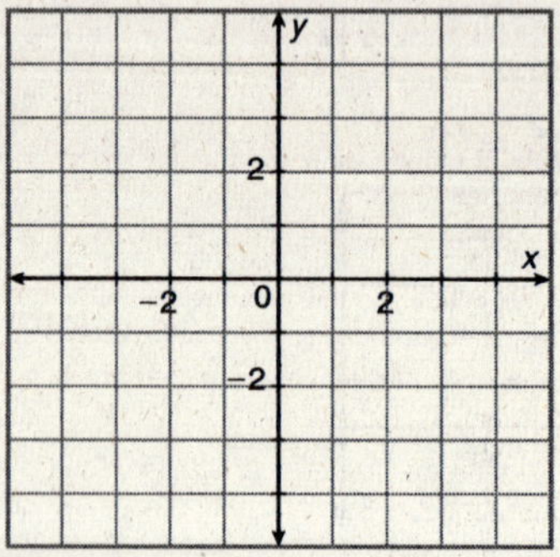

10. $P(1, 3)$, $Q(-2, 3)$, $R(-2, 1)$, $S(1, 0)$; x-axis

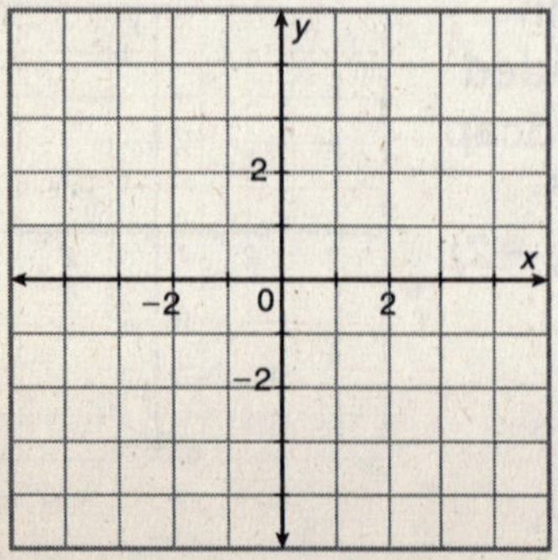

11. $J(3, -4)$, $K(1, -1)$, $L(-1, -1)$, $M(-2, -4)$; $y = x$

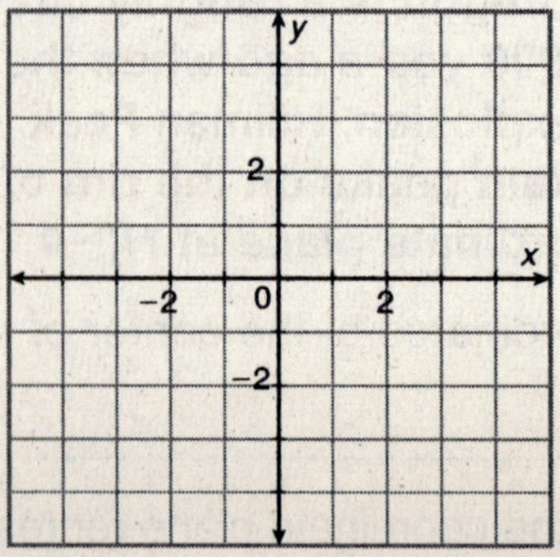

Name ______________________ Date ____________ Class ____________

LESSON 12-2

Practice B

Translations

Tell whether each transformation appears to be a translation.

1. 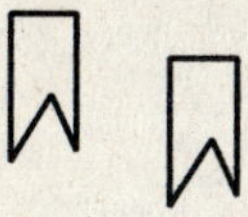 ________

2.  ________

3.  ________

4. 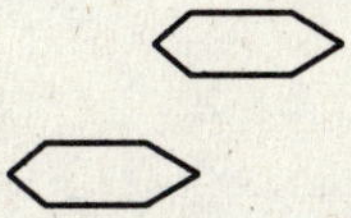 ________

Draw the translation of each figure along the given vector.

5. 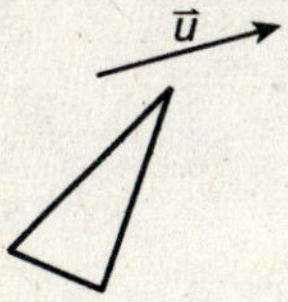

6. 

Translate the figure with the given vertices along the given vector.

7. $A(-1, 3)$, $B(1, 1)$, $C(4, 4)$; $\langle 0, -5\rangle$

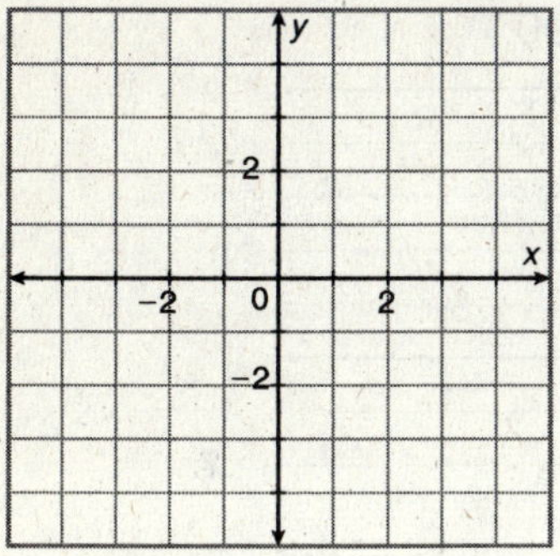

8. $P(-1, 2)$, $Q(0, 3)$, $R(1, 2)$, $S(0, 1)$; $\langle 1, 0\rangle$

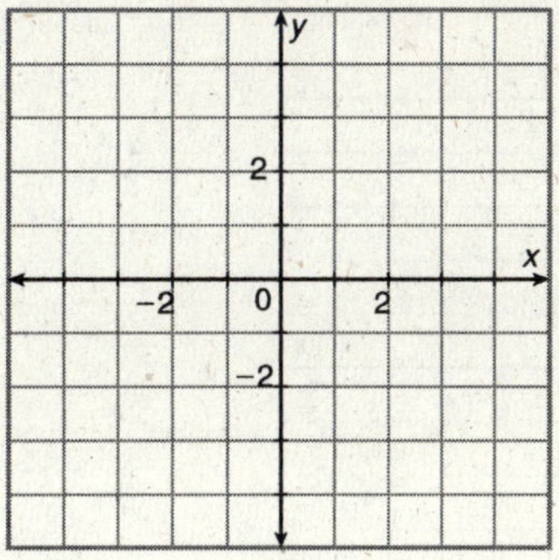

9. $L(3, 2)$, $M(1, -3)$, $N(-2, -2)$; $\langle -2, 3\rangle$

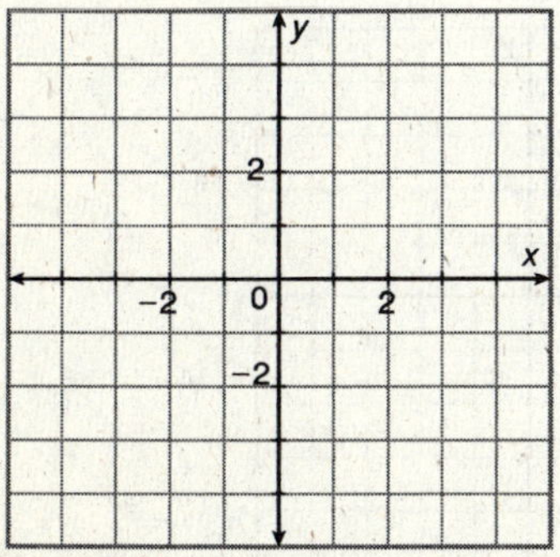

10. $D(2, -2)$, $E(2, -4)$, $F(1, -4)$, $G(-2, -2)$; $\langle 2, 5\rangle$

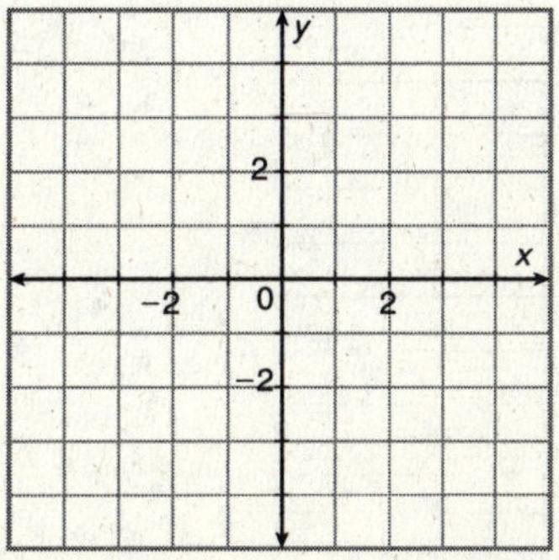

11. A builder is trying to level out some ground with a front-end loader. He picks up some excess dirt at (9, 16) and then maneuvers through the job site along the vectors $\langle -6, 0\rangle$, $\langle 2, 5\rangle$, and $\langle 8, 10\rangle$ to get to the spot to unload the dirt. Find the coordinates of the unloading point. Find a single vector from the loading point to the unloading point.

____

Name ______________________ Date ____________ Class ____________

LESSON 12-3

Practice B

Rotations

Tell whether each transformation appears to be a rotation.

1.  ________

2. 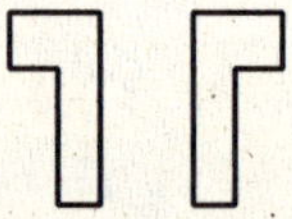 ________

3. 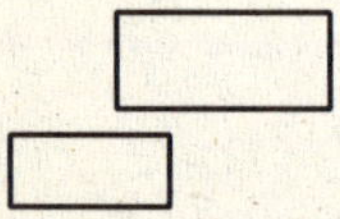 ________

4. 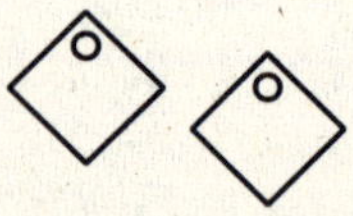 ________

Draw the rotation of each figure about point *P* by m∠*A*.

5. 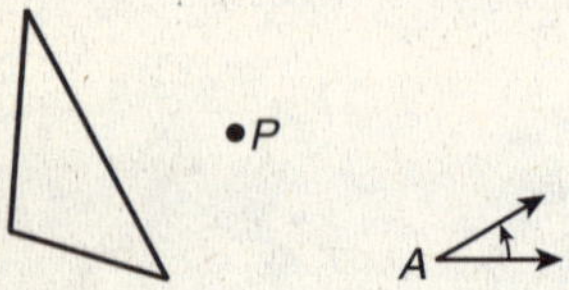

6. 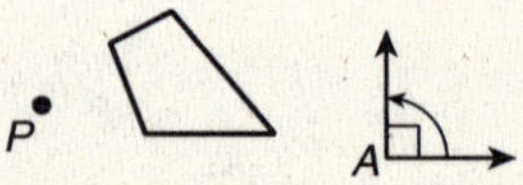

Rotate the figure with the given vertices about the origin using the given angle of rotation.

7. $A(-2, 3)$, $B(3, 4)$, $C(0, 1)$; 90°

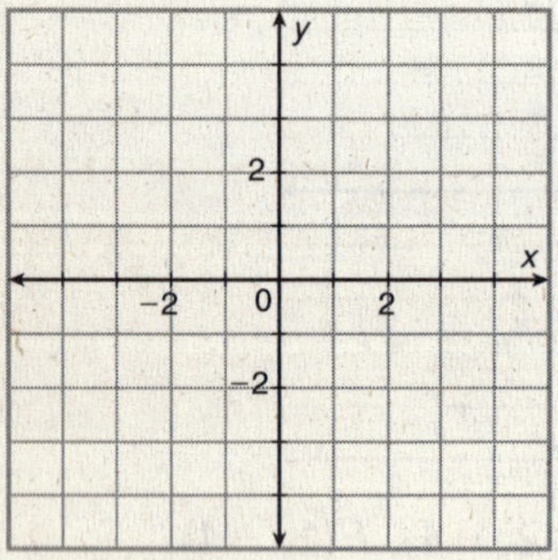

8. $D(-3, 2)$, $E(-4, 1)$, $F(-2, -2)$, $G(-1, -1)$; 90°

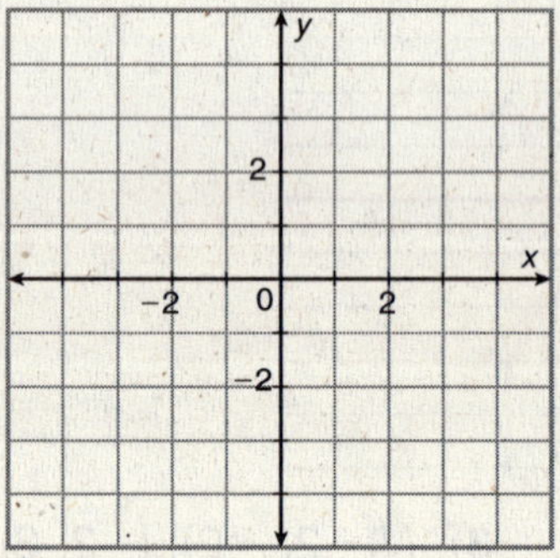

9. $J(2, 3)$, $K(3, 3)$, $L(1, -2)$; 180°

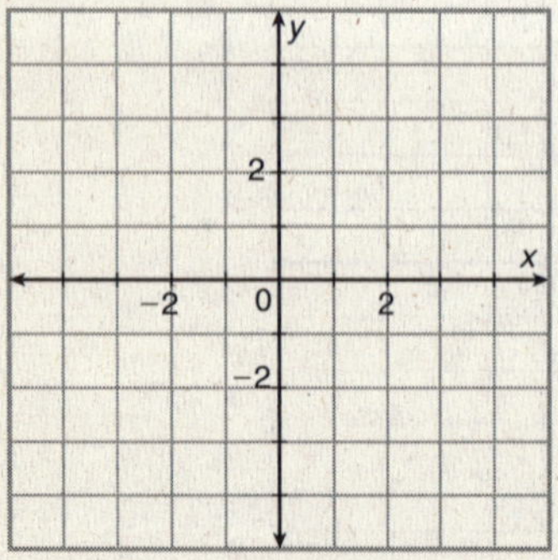

10. $P(0, 4)$, $Q(0, 1)$, $R(-2, 2)$, $S(-2, 3)$; 180°

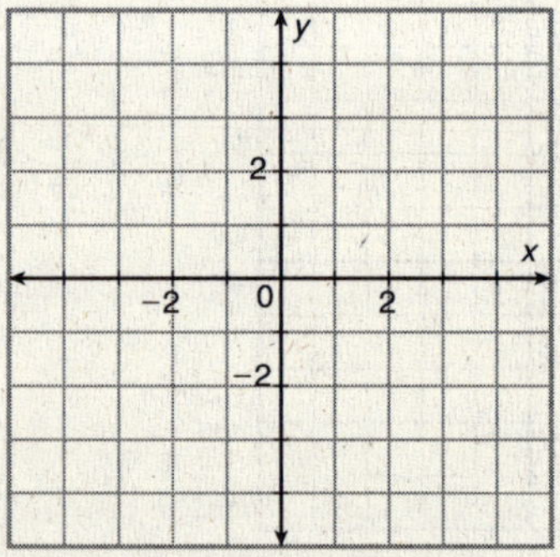

11. The steering wheel on Becky's car has a 15-inch diameter, and its center is at (0, 0). Point *X* at the top of the wheel has coordinates (0, 7.5). To turn left off her street, Becky must rotate the steering wheel by 300°. Find the coordinates of *X* when the steering wheel is rotated. Round to the nearest tenth. (*Hint:* How many degrees short of a full rotation is 300°?) ____________

Name ______________________ Date ____________ Class ____________

LESSON 12-4

Practice B

Compositions of Transformations

Draw the result of each composition of isometries.

1. Rotate $\triangle XYZ$ 90° about point P and then translate it along $\vec{v}$.

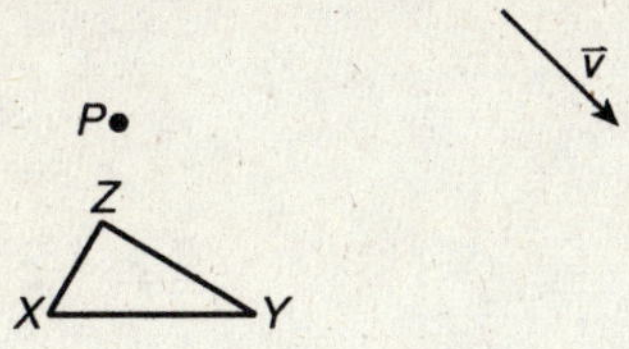

2. Reflect $\triangle LMN$ across line q and then translate it along $\vec{u}$.

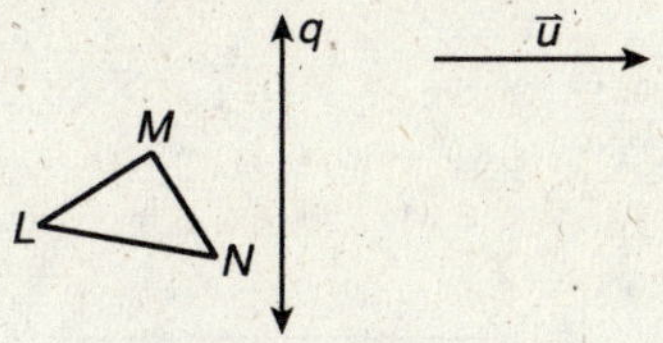

3. $ABCD$ has vertices $A(-3, 1)$, $B(-1, 1)$, $C(-1, -1)$, and $D(-3, -1)$. Rotate $ABCD$ 180° about the origin and then translate it along the vector $\langle 1, -3 \rangle$.

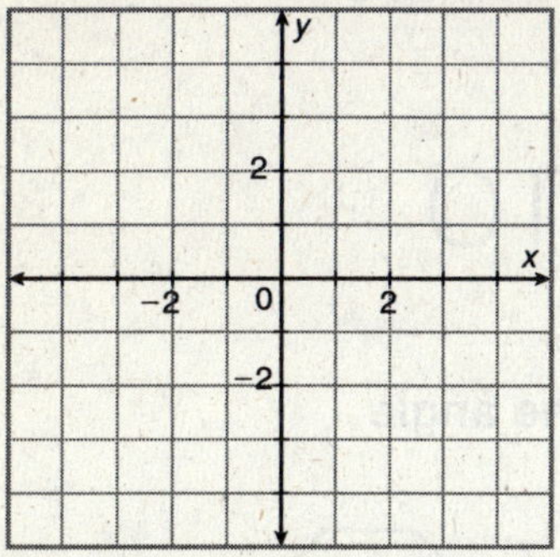

4. $\triangle PQR$ has vertices $P(1, -1)$, $Q(4, -1)$, and $R(3, 1)$. Reflect $\triangle PQR$ across the x-axis and then reflect it across $y = x$.

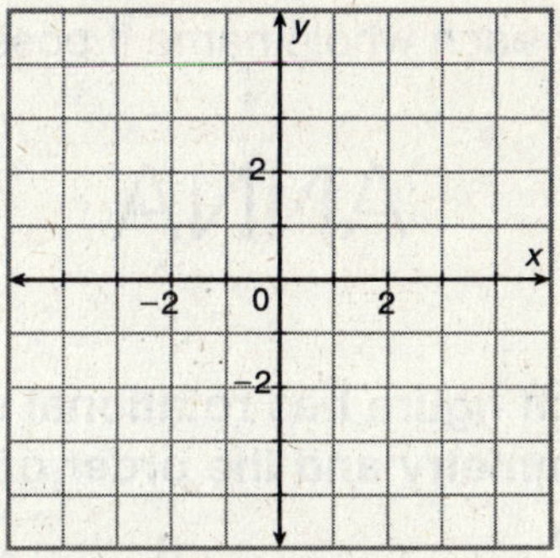

5. Ray draws equilateral $\triangle EFG$. He draws two lines that make a 60° angle through the triangle's center. Ray wants to reflect $\triangle EFG$ across ℓ_1 and then across ℓ_2. Describe what will be the same and what will be different about the image of $\triangle E''F''G''$ compared to $\triangle EFG$.

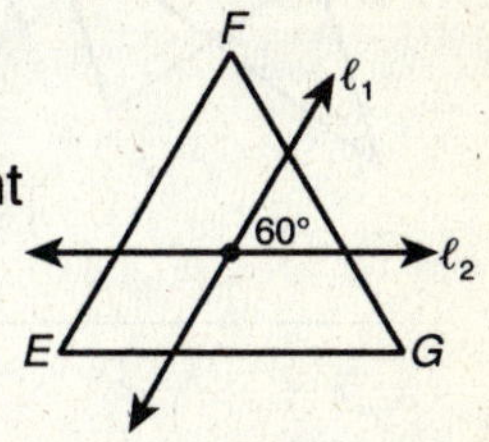

____

____

____

Draw two lines of reflection that produce an equivalent transformation for each figure.

6. translation: $STUV \rightarrow S'T'U'V'$

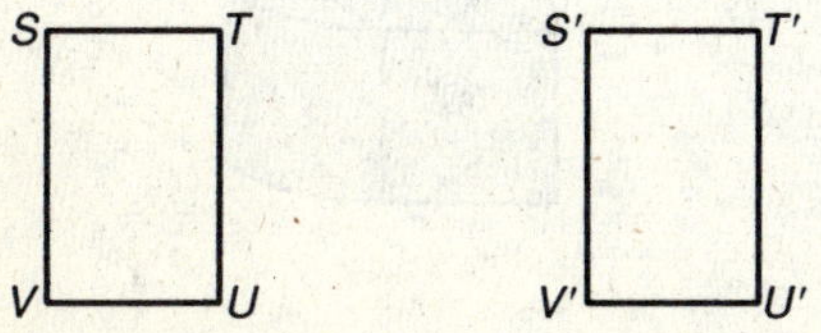

7. rotation with center P: $STUV \rightarrow S'T'U'V'$

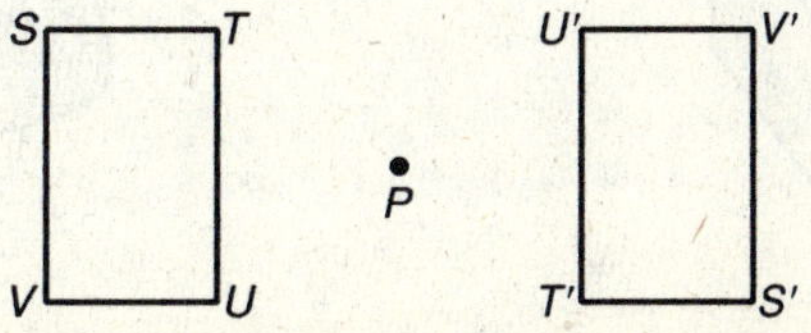

Name ______________________________ Date ____________ Class ____________

LESSON 12-5

Practice B

Symmetry

Tell whether each figure has line symmetry. If so, draw all lines of symmetry.

1. 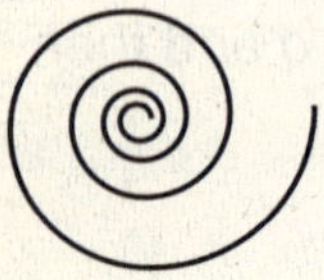 ____________

2. 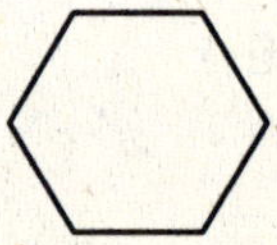 ____________

3.  ____________

4. Anna, Bob, and Otto write their names in capital letters. Draw all lines of symmetry for each whole name if possible.

ANNA BOB OTTO

Tell whether each figure has rotational symmetry. If so, give the angle of rotational symmetry and the order of the symmetry.

5.  ____________

6. 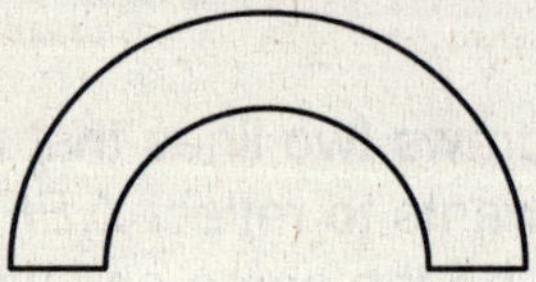 ____________

7. 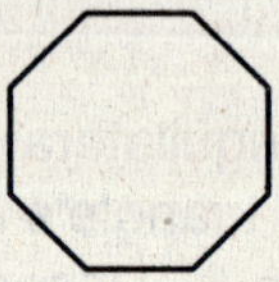 ____________

8. This figure shows the Roman symbol for Earth. Draw all lines of symmetry. Give the angle and order of any rotational symmetry.

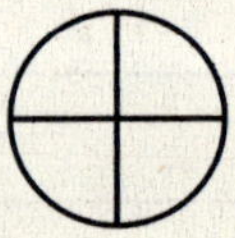

____

Tell whether each figure has plane symmetry, symmetry about an axis, both, or neither.

9. 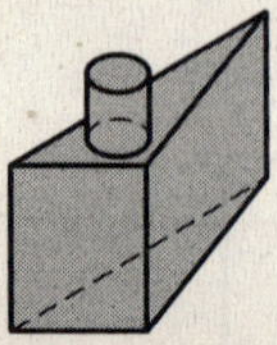 ____________

10. 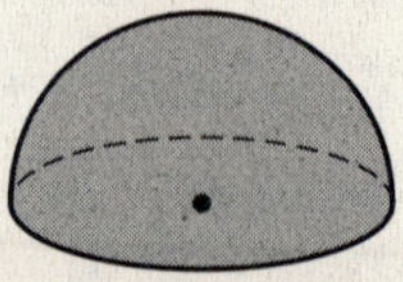 ____________

11. 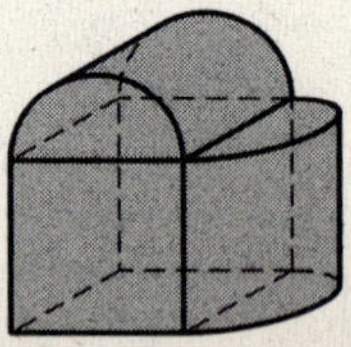 ____________

Name ______________________ Date ____________ Class ____________

LESSON **12-6**

Practice B

Tessellations

Tell whether each pattern has translation symmetry, glide reflection symmetry, or both.

1.

____

2.

____

3.

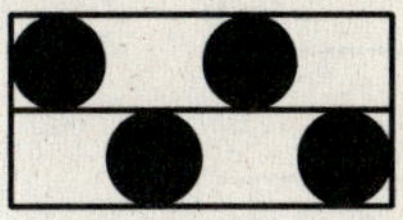

____

Use the given figure to create a tessellation.

4.

5.

Classify each tessellation as regular, semiregular, or neither.

6.

____

7.

____

8.

____

Determine whether the given regular polygon(s) can be used to form a tessellation. If so, draw the tessellation.

9.

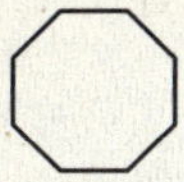

____

10.

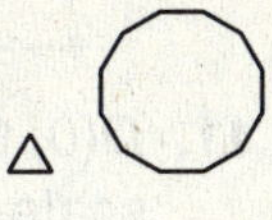

____

11.

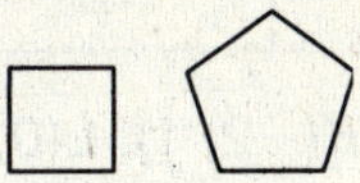

____

Name ______________________ Date ______________ Class ______________

LESSON 12-7

Practice B
Dilations

Tell whether each transformation appears to be a dilation.

1. 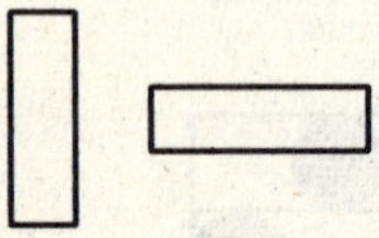 ________

2. 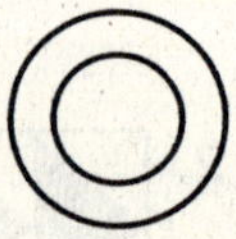 ________

3. 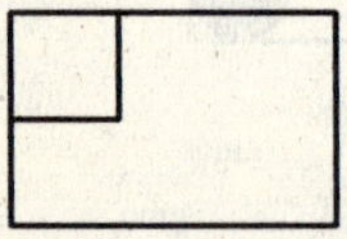 ________

4. 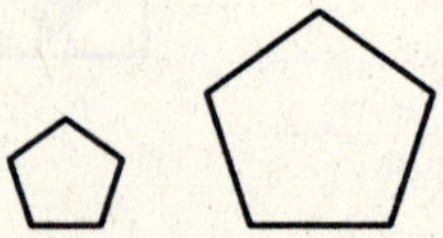 ________

Draw the dilation of each figure under the given scale factor with center of dilation *P*.

5. scale factor: $\frac{1}{2}$

6. scale factor: -2

7. A sign painter creates a rectangular sign for Mom's Diner on his computer desktop. The desktop version is 12 inches by 4 inches. The actual sign will be 15 feet by 5 feet. If the capital *M* in "Mom's" will be 4 feet tall, find the height of the *M* on his desktop version. ________________

Draw the image of the figure with the given vertices under a dilation with the given scale factor centered at the origin.

8. $A(2, -2)$, $B(2, 3)$, $C(-3, 3)$, $D(-3, -2)$; scale factor: $\frac{1}{2}$

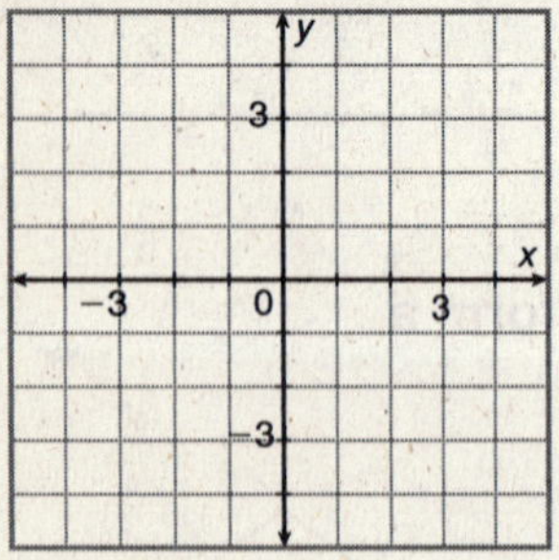

9. $P(-4, 4)$, $Q(-3, 1)$, $R(2, 3)$; scale factor: -1

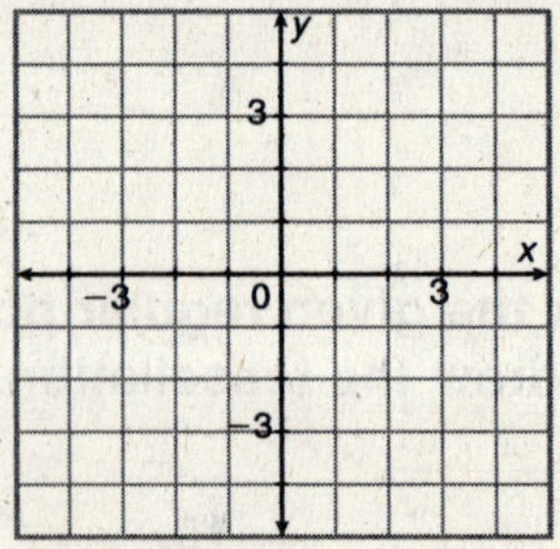

10. $J(0, 2)$, $K(-2, 1)$, $L(0, -2)$, $M(2, -1)$; scale factor: 2

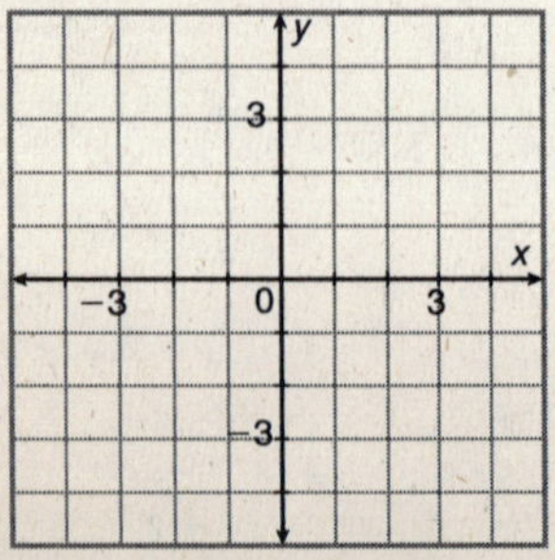

11. $D(0, 0)$, $E(-1, 0)$, $F(-1, -1)$; scale factor: -2

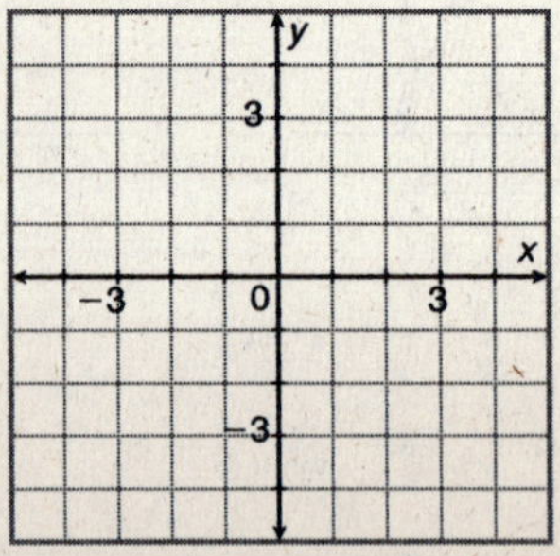